Handpainted
Gifts *for* ALL OCCASIONS

Kerry Trout

NORTH LIGHT BOOKS

CINCINNATI, OHIO

WWW.ARTISTSNETWORK.COM

About the Author

Kerry is a self-taught artist who has been painting since she was a child. She is the author of three North Light books: *Handpainting Your Furniture, From Flea Market to Fabulous* and *Decorative Mini Murals You Can Paint*. Kerry is a DecoArt Helping Artist and has recently joined the few decorative artist trailblazers who are now selling their projects on CD-ROM. "It's the pattern packet of the future," she promises. "With a hundred pages and pictures, color swatches and other tools, it's more bang for the buck; CD-ROMs leave the old-fashioned pattern packet in the dust."

Kerry developed Liquid Shadow, the first product of its kind for decorative painting. Liquid Shadow is a water-based medium that enables painters to easily paint cast shadows and to deepen shading. It is fast becoming a must-have for artists. For more information about Liquid Shadow, contact Kerry at her studio, Studio on The Square, located at 59 W. Marion St., Danville, Indiana 46122, where she also teaches decorative painting classes and paints commissioned work. You can view more of Kerry's work by visiting her website: www.kerrytrout.com.

Published by North Light Books, an imprint of F&W Publications, Inc., 4700 Galbraith Road, Cincinnati, Ohio 45236. (800) 289-0963. First edition.

Other fine North Light Books are available from your local bookstore or art supply store, or direct from the publisher.

07 06 05 04 03   5 4 3 2 1

Library of Congress Cataloging-in-Publication Data

Trout, Kerry
    Handpainted gifts for all occasions / by Kerry Trout
        p. cm.
    ISBN 1-58180-426-1 (pbk. : alk. paper)
        1. Painting. 2. Decoration and ornament. 3. Gifts. I. Title.

TT385.T77 2004
745.7'23--dc21   2003054191

Editors: Gina Rath and Chris Read
Production Coordinator: Kristen Heller
Designer: Wendy Dunning
Photographers: Christine Polomsky and Tim Grondin

METRIC CONVERSION CHART

To convert	to	multiply by
Inches	Centimeters	2.54
Centimeters	Inches	0.4
Feet	Centimeters	30.5
Centimeters	Feet	0.03
Yards	Meters	0.9
Meters	Yards	1.1
Sq. Inches	Sq. Centimeters	6.45
Sq. Centimeters	Sq. Inches	0.16
Sq. Feet	Sq. Meters	0.09
Sq. Meters	Sq. Feet	10.8
Sq. Yards	Sq. Meters	0.8
Sq. Meters	Sq. Yards	1.2
Pounds	Kilograms	0.45
Kilograms	Pounds	2.2
Ounces	Grams	28.3
Grams	Ounces	0.035

In loving memory of Grover Cook

My biggest fan,

my friend,

my Dad

Acknowledgments

Jan Brooks ✳ Brenda Bush ✳ Amy Callihan ✳ Sarah Clark ✳

Kathy Cook ✳ Katie Cook ✳ Robert & Rosalie Craine ✳

Bobby Houser ✳ Kathy Kipp ✳ Christine Polomsky ✳ Gina

Rath ✳ Patti Luc-Rettig ✳ Rosemary Reynolds ✳ Joyce Rogers

✳ Laurie Sattler ✳ Ron & Judy Schweitzer ✳ Sharon Spencer

✳ Tom Trout

Table of Contents

Vicki & Gary
June 4, 1979

Agatha & Frank
March 26, 1953

Introduction

Giving is one of life's little pleasures for me. I have always put forth special thought into the gifts that I give, preferring to make rather than buy them. If you are a decorative painter, I'm sure your friends expect and appreciate something hand-painted from you as well. Sometimes I spend days painting a gift, but when I need a last minute present, I have acquired a treasure-trove of designs for beautiful and easy projects that I can complete in just a couple of hours.

Recently, when thinking about all of the things I have painted in the past, I realized that I have created a project for just about every gift-giving occasion there is. This book is the culmination of those thoughts: a book filled with painting projects for any season and any gift-giving opportunity that comes around, including lots of Quick Projects for those last-minute gift quandaries!

I'm excited to be able to share with you all of the projects that I have designed. I want you to have your own little treasure-trove of projects ready for any occasion and available for you with just the turn of a page.

In the 17 painting projects in this book, you will find lots of great gift ideas for those special people on your list: new babies, children's birthdays, weddings, Mother's Day, Father's Day, Easter, Valentine's Day and many others. But you'll find these projects are easily adaptable for other occasions as well. The Mother's Day Pillow, for example, will be just as grand a gift for Grandma's birthday, a niece's wedding shower, or for a thoughtful get-well gift.

When you need a project that is especially quick to paint, just flip through the book and look for those marked "Quick Projects."

I know you will enjoy hand-painting personal gifts for all the special occasions of your life.

Supplies *and* Basic Techniques

VALUABLE INFORMATION

Please read all directions before starting any of the projects in this book. I will not only give you clear instructions, but I will also explain why something is done in a specific way. I won't assume you can read between the lines. Also, don't skip a step in the directions. You may think you can cut corners (and perhaps you can in some cases); but for best results, I recommend following the instructions.

For the projects in this book, I used DecoArt Americana acrylic paints, but feel free to use the equivalent colors in other brands, or even to change colors to your liking. This book is a guide—use your artistic license to add your own personality to any project.

Gather all the supplies before you start painting. You don't want to be in the middle of a project and realize you have to run out to the hardware or craft store. Below is a list of basic supplies I keep on hand for painting. You may find that you already have many of these around the house.

Get a toolbox or tote to hold the supplies and keep them in one place. Craft stores have all kinds of wonderful boxes and containers made specifically for the artist and crafter.

You will most likely use many of these projects for gifts, but don't be too eager to wrap them up in pretty paper right away! You must allow a curing (complete drying) time after you have applied the final coat of varnish. And be sure to always sign your beautiful artwork; it will mean even more to the recipient.

BRUSHES

Buy the best brushes you can afford and treat them well. There are several excellent manufacturers of artist's brushes; I recommend buying a reputable brand. For

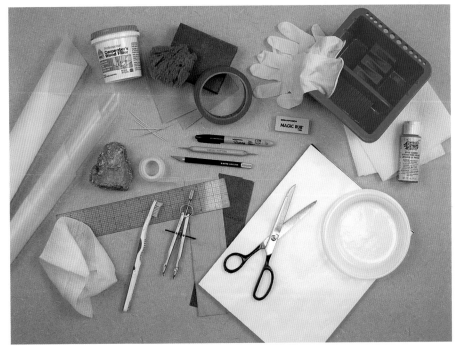

Suggested Supplies

Magic Rub® white eraser • Transfer paper, dark and light • Tracing paper • Stylus • Paper towels • Sandpaper • Tack cloth • Palettes • Water basin • Scotch tape • Low-tack painter's tape • C-thru® ruler • Compass • Right angle • Scissors • Craft knife • Permanent black marker • Freezer paper • Waxed paper • Pencil • Wood putty • Brush cleaner • Old toothbrush • Round toothpicks

the projects in this book, I used Loew-Cornell brushes; I like their quality and ability to spring back after a lot of use. Loew-Cornell has many brushes of all types—from an inexpensive line of beginner's craft brushes to high-end brushes for the professional artist.

Acrylic paint is very hard on brushes, so clean them thoroughly after each use. There are some very effective brush cleaners on the market. Some, such as the one I use, "The Masters" Brush Cleaner and Preserver by General Pencil Company, will remove even dried paint from the brush.

Once in a while, no matter how well you think you're cleaning your brushes, paint will get up into the ferrule (the metal band that holds the bristles) and it won't be easy to get out; this is called tunneling or fish mouth. The dried paint causes the bristles to separate and splay out, which ruins the shape of the brush and makes painting a struggle. When this happens, you can dip the ailing brush bristles (just the bristles) into boiling water for a few seconds, then lay the brush on a paper towel. The bristles will reshape themselves and the brush will get a second lease on life. I still use a few brushes left over from my college days. Because I've taken care of them, these 28-year-old brushes still retain their shape. You pay good money for brushes, so keep them as long as you can.

CARING FOR YOUR BRUSHES

One of the best ways you can take care of your brushes is to never, ever stand them in the water basin. (If you do this in my class, you'll get scolded!) This is a bad habit to get into; it will ruin brushes quickly. For one thing, it misshapes the bristles. But even worse, the brush acts as a wick; if the handle is wood, water can work its way up through the brush to damage the handle.

Change the water often. If you are rinsing the brush in cloudy gray water, your brush is not getting very clean.

Use brush cleaner at the end of each painting session. You can even leave some brush cleaners (check the instructions on the cleaner bottle) in the brush overnight to work on tough, dried-on paint or to condition the bristles.

After cleaning, lay the brushes flat on a paper towel until completely dry. Never stand them on end (bristles up) to dry. Also, don't put brushes away wet. Once the brushes are completely dry, you can then stand them on end for storage.

LIFE CYCLE OF A PAINT BRUSH

If you understand the life cycle of a paint brush you can keep it indefinitely. Some brushes can take on different roles as they get older; therefore, I seldom toss a brush into the trash.

When flat shaders are in good condition, they are excellent for floating colors or for double loading paint. But since acrylics are hard on them, eventually they will become tunneled or fish-mouthed, as mentioned previously. If, after cleaning and boiling the bristles, you are unable to return the brush to its original state, you can then demote the brush to its new role as a basecoater.

After using the brush as a basecoater for a while, you may notice the bristles getting worn; that means it's time for another new role for this brush. Turn the brush over and use the handle end for making dip-dots or for stirring.

It's a good idea to designate a few flat shaders for floating only.

Round brushes have a similar life cycle; however, when they become worn and misshapen, they become scruffies. A scruffy is a brush you will love! Scruffy brushes are just what they sound like: brushes that have worn out and become scruffy and out-of-shape. Used with an up-and-down pouncing motion they can make terrific trees and other foliage.

TRANSFER PAPER

There are several brands of transfer (or

graphite) paper on the market. This product is used like carbon paper—you put the paper face down between the surface you are going to paint and the pattern. When you trace over the pattern lines with a stylus or pencil, the transfer paper will "transfer" the marks onto the surface.

Transfer paper is a must for decorative painters. One sheet can be used over and over again. One thing to note, however, is that when graphite paper is new from the package, it's prone to be laden with graphite and sometimes this can smudge the painting surface. Smudges from some brands are more difficult to remove than others. To minimize this problem, lay the new graphite paper on the table (graphite side up) and lightly rub off the excess graphite powder with a soft cloth or paper towel, taking care not to tear the paper.

To make graphite paper easier to work with, cut it down to the size of the pattern you are transferring.

TRACING PAPER

Tracing paper is another staple of the painter's studio. Tracing paper is a thin, see-through paper, sold in tablets or on rolls. Tracing paper is sometimes called vellum (although true vellum is usually heavier and more expensive).

I use tracing paper all the time in order to maintain the quality of the original patterns. For instance, you can use tracing paper so you don't have to cut the patterns out from the pages of this book. Lay tracing paper over the pattern, tape it in place and trace the pattern using a pencil or fine-tip black marker. (Ballpoint pens don't work well on tracing paper.)

Here's a helpful tip: trace the pattern with a red marker, then use a pencil to transfer the pattern to the surface. It will be easier for you to see what you have traced.

TRANSFERRING PATTERNS

Using waxed paper is another way of saving the pattern from overuse. Lay the transfer paper (graphite side down) onto the painting surface with the pattern on top of the graphite paper, then use low-tack painter's tape to attach them to the surface.

Cut a piece of waxed paper the size of the pattern, and tape this on top of the pattern (see page 68). As you trace over the waxed paper, the white lines you make show what you have already traced. I recommend using a stylus if you use the waxed paper method of transferring patterns.

REPOSITIONING PATTERNS

Some of my project instructions will ask you to reposition a pattern. This can be tricky if you can't see through the pattern onto the painted surface. I want to make this as easy as possible for you; if you don't get the pattern positioned exactly where it was the first time, the final artwork could look inaccurate.

Here's what to do to make the job effortless:

* Look at the pattern and find the registration marks printed on it, or make your own marks; then transfer the registration marks when you transfer the pattern.
* Cut around the pattern to remove excess paper but don't cut off the registration marks. Instead, cut away just half of the marks by cutting down the dotted line.
* When you need to reposition the pattern, line up the half-marks on the pattern with the registration mark on the painted surface. Your pattern will be precisely in its original position.

RESOURCES

Many of the surfaces for the projects in this book can be found in your local craft, outlet or discount stores, but I found a few of the pieces online. See page 142 for a list of excellent sources for project surfaces.

Floating

1 Always use the largest brush possible when floating (flat shaders are good for floating). Dip the brush into clean water; take it out and touch the bristles to a paper towel. Let the water wick out until the shine is off of the bristles, this leaves enough water in the bristles for floating.

2 Dip one corner into the paint.

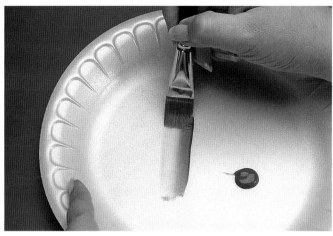

3 Immediately swipe the brush back-and-forth across the palette about eight times until you see the color float across the bristles. You'll have to bear down on the bristles until they bend, otherwise the paint won't flow across the bristles properly.

4 Notice the gradation of color from dark to transparent. You are now ready to float the paint onto your project.

Double Float

Load the brush the same way you did for floating (see step 1, previous page). Stroke on a float in one direction then flip the brush and stroke on a second float right next to the first.

Drybrush

It's difficult to drybrush with a brand new brush, so use a brush that is somewhat worn. Load it with paint, then wipe it off on a paper towel. You will use the paint that is left on the brush to drybrush. Drag the bristles across the surface and you'll see "dry" streaks of paint. The brushstroke should skip and be rough-looking.

Pulled Leaf Stroke

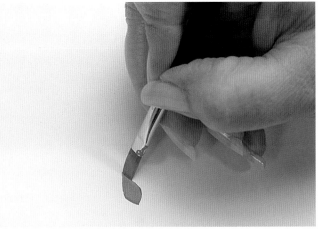

1 Load a flat brush with paint. Begin the stroke by touching the brush to the surface at an angle, as shown.

2 Push down on the brush to make the bristles flare a bit, then pull, turn and lift to a point. The point of the brush closest to you will form the base or stem of the leaf, while the opposite edge will turn slightly and end up making the tip of the leaf.

Stroke Petal

Begin by making a little center dot for a guide. Load a flat brush. Use the same stroke as for the pulled leaf, above. Turn your work so that each petal stroke pulls in to the center dot.

Curlicues or Tendrils

To make successful curlicues, first learn the correct way to use a liner brush. When using a liner or a script liner, it is imperative to use very thinned paint—which means lots of water! That's the reason liners have long bristles—they are designed to hold enough paint to execute a very long stroke. And if you load the brush properly—up to the ferrule—you'll be surprised how far each stroke goes before the paint runs out. Just be sure that the paint is thin enough to glide off the bristles.

Here's how I demonstrate to my students the correct way to load and use a script liner: I tell them I can write the entire alphabet in one stroke. Of course they laugh—until they see me do it! So keep this in mind: a skinny brush needs skinny paint!

1 Load thinned medium green paint onto a no. 1 liner and paint a free-flowing tendril. Hold your brush on the ferrule for control and angle it almost straight up and down (perpendicular to the surface) while painting.

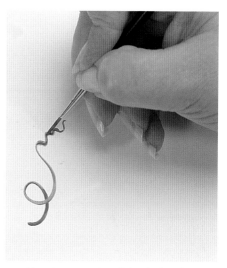

2 Use the same brush loaded with a darker green to shade the tendril.

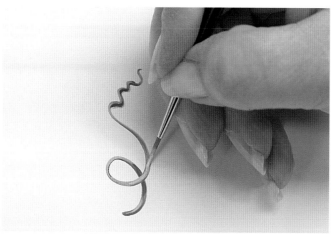

3 Add highlighting with the same brush loaded with a lighter green.

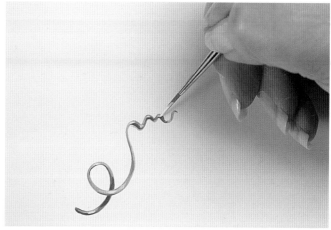

4 Add a touch of thinned white on the curves for a final highlight.

Damp Blending

"Damp blending" is using a clean, damp brush to soften the hard edge of a paint stroke while it is still wet. I use this technique when floating won't make a wide enough blended area.

For an easy little practice lesson, try painting this cherry. You will be using three values.

1) Begin by basecoating the cherry with Santa Red (the middle value) using a no. 4 flat shader. You will need two coats.

2) Apply a circle of Cadmium Red (the light value) to the roundest part of the cherry. Rinse your brush and blot it until it is just damp. Now stroke over the outside edge of the Cadmium Red highlight. Keep your brush perpendicular to the edge of the highlight. Go around the circle until the color is blended, being sure to leave the very center untouched.

3) Now apply a crescent-shaped stroke of Black Plum (the dark value) to the lower edge of the cherry. This is the shading. Again, rinse your brush, blot it, and diffuse the hard edge on the inside with the clean, damp brush.

Notice how the blended values seem to disappear into the middle value basecoat. By blending those values you made a flat shape appear to be three dimensional.

Let me stress again the importance of keeping the light value (highlighting) and dark value (shading) separated by the middle value. If the highlighting touches the shading, the illusion is lost. This separation is the key to adding dimension and realism to your artwork.

Middle value
(basecoat)

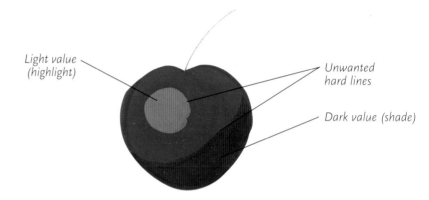

Light value
(highlight)

Unwanted
hard lines

Dark value (shade)

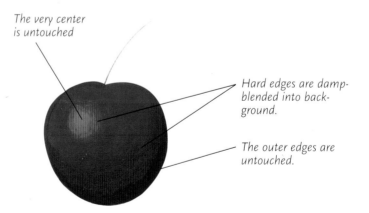

The very center
is untouched

Hard edges are damp-
blended into back-
ground.

The outer edges are
untouched.

Using a Rake Brush

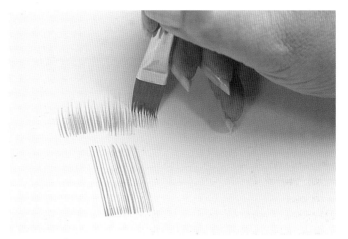

1 A rake brush is sometimes called a comb. It is a specialty brush designed to paint very fine hair and grasses. It can do this because the ends of the bristles do not come to a sharp flat edge but are thin and staggered. There are enough bristles in the body of the brush to hold the paint, yet the paint flows onto the surface from very fine individual end-hairs that are longer than all the other hairs. Paint needs to be extremely thin to flow from these fine hairs, in order to get the desired look. In fact, the rake brush is so delicate that it simply won't perform if the paint is too thick.

2 To paint hair or fur, load thinned paint onto the rake brush. Hold the brush perpendicular to the surface and, very lightly, just touch the very end of the bristles onto the surface. Then pull down with short, quick strokes. Lift to a taper as you end the stroke. When painting grass, always start the stroke at the bottom (ground) and "flick" your brush upward (skyward).

Double Loading

To double load a brush, place two colors of paint close together onto the palette . Run the flat side of the brush down the middle so that each edge of the brush picks up color. As you did for floating, wipe the brush back and forth on your palette. Repeat until the colors meet each other in the middle of the bristles. Now you are ready to apply the paint to the surface.

Ruffled Petal Flowers

Begin with a double-loaded flat brush. Touch the brush onto the surface and wiggle the brush as you slide, while you turn or pivot the brush. Continue this wiggle stroke around the center of the flower. Turn your work to make the stroke easier. End the stroke on the chisel edge (tip end) of the brush.

PROJECT 1

Snowshoe *Hare in Winter*

A nyone who knows me can attest to my passion for painting rabbits. So when I found this old coal bucket in an antique store, I knew I had to paint a rabbit on it. And a snowshoe hare with winterberries is the perfect painting project for a snowy day in January. The project would be a great winter housewarming gift for a new homeowner to display next to her fireplace.

MATERIALS

Loew-Cornell Brushes

Series 7300 no. 4, 6 and 10 shaders

Series 7350 no. 1 and 10/0 liners

Series 7520 ¼-inch (6mm) and ½-inch (12mm) filbert rakes

Series 7550 ½-inch (12mm) wash

Additional Supplies

DecoArt Americana Ebony Black spray paint

tracing paper

white chalk pencil or soapstone

cotton swabs

DecoArt Star Lite Topcoat

DecoArt Americana Spray Sealer (DAS 13: matte)

toothpicks

low-tack painter's tape

wire brush

Surface

Coal bucket (from an antique store)

Paint

DecoArt Americana Acrylics

Blue Chiffon

Lamp (Ebony) Black

Napa Red

Heritage Brick

Asphaltum

Sable Brown

Cool White

Gingerbread

Summer Lilac + French Grey Blue (3:1)

Summer Lilac

French Grey Blue

Titanium (Snow) White

Summer Lilac + Napa Red + Sable Brown (2:1:1)

Dark undercoat = French Grey Blue + Summer Lilac (2:1)

Light undercoat = Titanium (Snow) White + Dark under- coat mixture (1:2)

Titanium (Snow) White + Heritage Brick (3:1)

17

Patterns

This pattern may be hand-traced or photo-copied for personal use only. Enlarge at 117% to bring it up to full size.

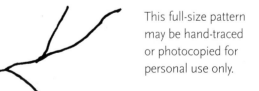

This full-size pattern may be hand-traced or photocopied for personal use only.

This pattern may be hand-traced or photocopied for personal use only. Enlarge at 125% to bring it up to full size.

Preparation and Basecoating

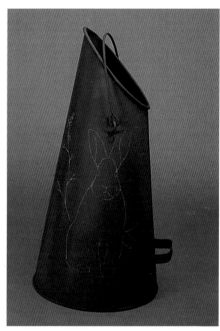

1 Make sure the surface is clean. Use a wire brush to remove any rust. Spray the bucket with two coats of Ebony Black acrylic spray paint. Allow the paint to dry between coats.

2 Enlarge or shrink the snowshoe hare pattern to fit your bucket, then transfer the pattern to tracing paper. Turn the tracing paper over and go over the lines using a white chalk pencil.

Hint ~ An alternative to a chalk pencil is a soapstone, which you can find in the sewing notions of your craft store.

3 Align the pattern, tape it to the bucket, then trace over it.

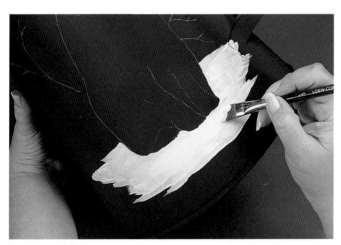

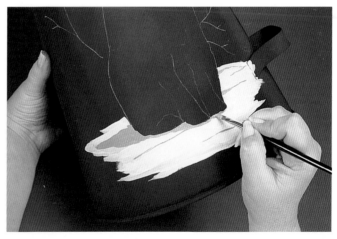

4 Use the ½-inch (12mm) wash brush to paint the first layer of Cool White. Stroke on some Titanium (Snow) White over the Cool White (mostly on the right side) then pull a little into the front area. Paint the sides with a ragged stroke to give a vignette effect.

5 Using your no. 6 shader with Summer Lilac and French Grey Blue (3:1), apply some shadows on the lower left side of the hare and underneath the feet in front. Also add a few streaks in the snow. Save a little of this mixture for use in step 11.

Winterberry Branches

6 Paint the branches in the background with Asphaltum using the chisel edge of your no. 6 shader.

7 With the chisel edge of the same brush, use Sable Brown to highlight the branches.

8 Add just a touch of Sable Brown to Titanium (Snow) White to make a light beige and, using the same brush, accent a few of the branches a little more.

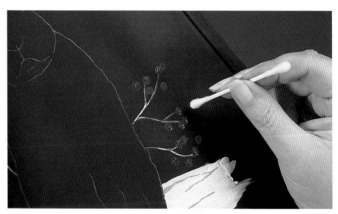

9 Use a cotton swab, with Napa Red, to dot in the first set of berries.

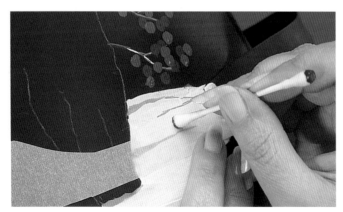

10 Use Heritage Brick on a cotton swab to dot in the second set of berries. Add a few fallen berries on the snow by laying a piece of tracing paper over the snow and then dotting on the berry, half on the paper and half on the snow. When you lift the paper it will look like half of the berry is in the snow.

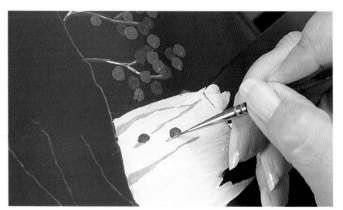

11 Use the no. 10/0 liner and the shadow color from step 5 to add a tiny shadow on the left side of each fallen berry.

Fur and Ears

12 Use a cotton swab and Gingerbread to touch in a few more berries. Highlight the Napa Red berries with a toothpick and a mixture of Titanium (Snow) White and Heritage Brick (3:1). The highlight goes on the upper right portion of the berries. The other berries are highlighted with Titanium (Snow) White, also using a toothpick.

13 Paint the darker undercoat of the fur with French Grey Blue and Summer Lilac (2:1), using your ½-inch (12mm) wash brush.

14 Paint the light undercoat section using the same brush with the dark undercoat mixture (from step 13) mixed with Titanium (Snow) White (2:1). You can leave the chin and mouth area uncovered to retain the lines.

15 Create a pale pink mixture with Summer Lilac, Napa Red and Sable Brown (2:1:1) and, using your ¼-inch (6mm) rake brush, paint the inside of the ears. (For tips on using the rake, see page 15.)

16 Thin Cool White, and with your ¼-inch (6mm) rake, sketch in hairs on the ears.

Ears and Face

17 Add a second layer of fur on the ears with thinned Titanium (Snow) White on your ¼-inch (6mm) rake. Also stroke in long hairs in front of the ears using the no. 1 liner.

18 Use thinned Sable Brown on your no. 4 shader and sketch in a few brown patches on the ears. Also use Asphaltum to tip the edges of the ears.

19 Use your rake and thinned Blue Chiffon to add fur over the dark undercoat. Use short strokes to paint the fur on the head.

20 Before painting near the nose, sketch in the nose lines if necessary.

21 Still using the ¼-inch (6mm) rake, apply thinned Cool White to the right side of the face on top of the light undercoat.

Face and Eyes

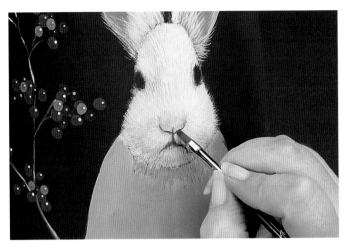

22 Thin Sable Brown, just as you did for the ears. Add touches of the Sable Brown around the nose and muzzle, with the chisel edge of a no. 4 shader. Use Asphaltum and the same brush to add detail around the nose and mouth.

23 With a 10/0 liner, stroke in tiny hairs around the eyes with Cool White. Also add thinned Titanium (Snow) White highlights to the right side of the face.

24 Use a 10/0 liner and Cool White to stroke in a few individual hairs over the mouth. Basecoat the eyes with Asphaltum on a no. 4 shader. While this is drying, use thinned Titanium (Snow) White on a 10/0 liner to bring out a few lashes above the eyes.

25 Load a no. 4 shader with Lamp (Ebony) Black to paint the pupils. With a 10/0 liner, add a tiny bit of French Grey Blue on the bottom of the eyeball for the fur reflecting in the eyeball.

Whiskers and Fur

26 Use a toothpick and Titanium (Snow) White to dot highlights onto the eyes. Load a no. 1 liner with thinned Titanium (Snow) White and add whiskers and brow hairs.

27 Moving on down to the snow hare's body, use thinned Cool White on a ½-inch (12mm) rake to stroke in fur over the light undercoat. These strokes are longer than the strokes on the head. Start at the neck and come down and out. The hairs need to overlap the black background a little to show the fur. When you get down to the toes, make the strokes very short again. The strokes should overlap the foot and the purple-shaded snow just a little bit.

28 On the darker undercoat, use Blue Chiffon and a ¼-inch (6mm) rake to finish adding the fur.

29 Load a ½-inch (12mm) rake with Titanium (Snow) White and add highlight hairs over top of only the lightest fur (which was painted with Cool White). Use the chisel edge of a no. 4 shader, with thinned Sable Brown, to shade the bottom edges of the feet. Use the flat edge of the shader to pull the brown up onto the toes, and the chisel edge to add the little spaces between the toes. With a 10/0 liner and Asphaltum, touch in little darker hairs around the bottoms of the feet.

Final Steps

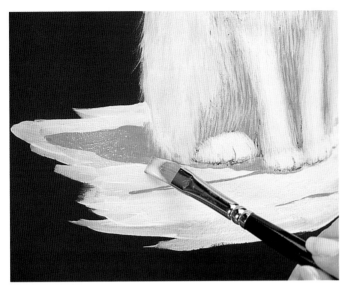

30 Add Star Lite Topcoat to the snow, using a no. 10 shader. You will need two coats of this since it is very subtle. Also dot some onto the berries.

31 Once everything is completely dry, spray a matte sealer over the whole piece to protect your painting.

Loving Greetings

Valentine's Day Candy Dish

*J*ere's a sweet Valentine's Day treat for Mom, Grandma or a special friend. Paint this beautiful candy dish in an afternoon, and she will enjoy it year round.

MATERIALS

Loew-Cornell Brushes

Series 7520 ½-inch (12mm) filbert rake

Series 7300 nos. 4 and 6 shaders

Series 7400 ½-inch (12mm) angular shader

Series 7350 no. 2 liner

Series 7000 nos. 1 and 3 rounds

Additional Supplies

1-inch (25mm) foam brush or basecoater

white chalk pencil

¼-inch (6mm) lace (optional)

fine grit sandpaper

DecoArt Americana All-Purpose Sealer

Surface

Candy dish from Painter's Paradise

Paint

DecoArt Americana Acrylics

Baby Pink

Titanium (Snow) White

Light Avocado

Citron Green

Burgundy Wine

Plantation Pine

Violet Haze

Patterns

This pattern may be hand-traced or photocopied for personal use only. Enlarge at 105% to bring it up to full size.

Stripes and Leaves

Sand the wooden lid with fine grit sandpaper, then seal it with wood sealer. Using a 1-inch (25mm) foam brush or bristle brush, apply two coats of Baby Pink. Allow the paint to dry thoroughly, and sand between coats.

With a white chalk pencil, mark off the lid with lines one inch (25mm) apart in both directions.

Thin Titanium (Snow) White and paint stripes in each direction, using the ½-inch (12mm) rake. Let dry. Go back and paint stripes in between the first set, in both directions. Allow to dry, then transfer the rose pattern onto the lid.

1 Basecoat the leaves, using the no. 6 shader and Light Avocado. Place the chisel edge of the no. 6 shader, loaded with Plantation Pine, on the outside left edge of the leaf and stroke inward, at an angle, toward the stem. This should be a very short stroke—almost a flick of the brush. Also with the chisel edge, draw a center line from the stem to the tip of the leaf. Starting at the base, make the same short strokes of shading, this time going outward toward the right side of the leaf.

2 Load the same brush with Citron Green and stroke on the highlights on the left side of the leaf, on top of the Light Avocado. (Don't allow the highlight color to touch the shade color. The Light Avocado must separate the two colors.) Make these strokes of highlighting run in the same direction as the first strokes of Plantation Pine (step 1).

3 Add a touch of Titanium (Snow) White to Citron Green to make a final highlight color. Brush this on top of the Citron Green highlights in the same manner and direction as the first highlight. This should be very small and only within the confines of the Citron Green strokes. Load the no. 2 liner with this same color (thinned with water) and paint the veins. To do this successfully, use the tip of the brush, start at the stem and drag out the center vein using less pressure as you near the tip of the leaf. Applying less pressure makes the line thinner. Go back to the base of the center vein and drag out veins on either side of the center. Arch the side veins slightly, making them thinner than the center vein. Complete all the leaves in this manner, except the two that are overlapping roses, then add tendrils (see page 13).

Roses

Please practice these rose strokes on paper before doing them on your project. These roses are painted with an angular shader. While angular shaders are great for certain applications, they are a bit different from ordinary flat shaders: they are angled like a kitchen broom to make them easier to handle. You don't have to hold the brush straight up and down to make certain strokes. The brush has short bristles on one side and longer bristles on the other, so I will refer to each side as either the heel (the short end) or the toe (the long end).

To achieve the rippled edges on the rose petals, wiggle the brush up and down just a little while painting each petal. I'll remind you to wiggle the brush through-out the steps.

To help you easily see which petal I am referring to, at the bottom of the next page I have labeled each petal on a finished rose.

Before beginning to paint, please refer to page 15 for directions on how to double load a brush.

1 Basecoat the roses with a thin coat of Burgundy Wine. Double load a ½-inch (12mm) angular shader with Burgundy Wine on the heel and Titanium (Snow) White on the toe. Load it so that you have more burgundy than white in the brush.

Petal 1. Start at the top-middle petal and center the brush so that the heel is at 6 o'clock and the toe is at 10 o'clock. Make a fan-like stroke (remember to wiggle the brush to form a ruffled edge), allowing the white to overlap the basecoat, while pivoting your brush so that the heel stays at 6 o'clock. Start and end your stroke so that the white forms a taper on the outside edges of the petal.

2 **Petals 2-3**.. Center your brush again under the first stroke, but a bit lower, and paint two smaller petals inside the first petal. Start and end the petals on the tapered edges of petal 1. Allow the third stroke to slightly overlap the second stroke.

3 **Petal 4**. Reload the brush, if necessary, with Burgundy Wine on the heel and Titanium (Snow) White on the toe. With the heel centered again, place the toe of the brush on the left tapered edge of petal 3. Bring the brush downward and curve it, with the white edge of the brush forming a curved bowl and the heel barely pivoting. (Remember to put a bit of a wiggle into the stroke to form the ruffled edges.) Since it is difficult to push an angled shader, you'll need to stop the stroke midway at the center of the petal, then place the brush onto the right edge of petal 3 and make the same stroke (just the opposite of the last stroke). The two strokes should meet at the center. Although this is a two-stroke petal, it should look like one continuous smile-shaped stroke.

4 **Petals 5-6**. Place the toe of the brush just on the left outside edge of petal 1, while keeping the heel of the brush toward the center. Press down on the brush slightly to make the bristles flare a bit. Wiggling the brush, bring the stroke down the side, arching a bit to form a C-shaped stroke. End the stroke when it is horizontal. Do the same on the right side.

5 **Petal 7**. Add another smile-shaped stroke to the center of the rose, just below petal 4. This is the same stroke as petal 4 so refer to step 3. The only difference is that this stroke will be wider, and you will connect the ends to the tapered ends of petal 1.

6 **Petals 8-9**. Reload the brush if necessary. Begin petal 8 with the toe of the brush at 9 o'clock and the heel centered as before. Press down to make the bristles flare a bit and bring the petal out and down, making sure to cover the basecoated edge. End the stroke at 7 o'clock. Petal 9 begins at 3 o'clock and ends at 5 o'clock.

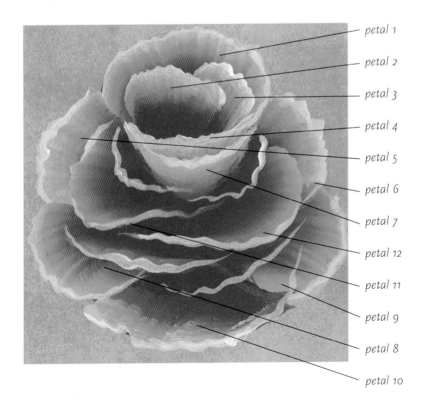

petal 1

petal 2

petal 3

petal 4

petal 5

petal 6

petal 7

petal 12

petal 11

petal 9

petal 8

petal 10

Roses, *continued*

7 Petal 10. You may be more comfortable turning your work to complete this stroke, since you'll need to keep the white edge of the petal on the outside (as you have done previously). With an angular shader, it can be awkward if you don't turn the surface and allow the toe to point away from you. Place the toe of the brush at the bottom edge of petal 8 and center the heel of the brush in the flower. With a wiggle, bring the brush toe around to form the front petal, and bring the heel across as well, taking care not to stroke over petal 8 too much. End the stroke right at the lower edge of petal 9, and use just the toe of the brush to make a taper. The last stroke may look awkward to you, but it will be hidden in the next steps.

8 Petals 11-12 Again, reload the brush and with the same ruffle-making wiggle, make two smaller petals in the center, flanking petal 7 (in the center of the rose). Deepen the color of the inside bowl of the rose and the shadows with Burgundy Wine on a no. 4 shader, then let dry.

9 With more pressure concentrated on the toe of the brush, stroke in one or two "slices" into the large spaces (the darkest areas). With Titanium (Snow) White loaded onto a no. 2 liner, apply wavy lines to the edges of the petals and onto the dark areas as well, to simulate the edges of more petals.

Lavender

1 Use a no. 2 liner to paint a thin stem and bud with Light Avocado. Dab in buds with Violet Haze on a no. 3 round. These are comma strokes with a slight arch to them.

2 Mix Titanium (Snow) White into the Violet Haze, and add some more buds. Switch to a no. 1 round brush loaded with Plantation Pine, and apply small comma strokes at the base of the buds.

1   2

If you like, finish off the lid with ¼-inch (6mm) lace around the rim .

PROJECT 3

Spring Table Runner

This delightful table runner can adorn your table throughout the spring months and will be a colorful complement to your centerpieces.

For this project you will be using DecoArt's newly formulated fabric paint—SoSoft Fabric Acrylics. They're wonderful to work with. There's no need to bother with adding fabric medium; because the paints have a longer open time (the time before the paint dries), you can easily blend colors. There's no need to scrub the paint into the fabric anymore. If you don't have fabric painting brushes, your other Loew-Cornell flats and liners will work fine.

Since the colors blend more easily when they are wet, plan to work on and complete one section of the project at a time. For example, rather than basecoating all the leaves for the whole project and then moving on to all the flowers, complete all the steps for one section at a time.

You may want to practice painting on some scrap pieces of fabric to get used to working with fabric paint.

MATERIALS

Loew-Cornell Fabric Painting Brushes
Series 223 nos. 4 and 6 shaders
Series 227 no. 4 liner
Series 226 no. 0 spotter

Additional Supplies
freezer paper
graphite paper
tracing paper
iron
pencil

Surface
Canvas table runner from
Bagworks

Paint
DecoArt SoSoft Fabric Acrylics

Avocado Green

Hauser Light Green

Hauser Dark Green

Dark Burgundy

White

Baby Pink Deep

Primary Yellow

Pineapple

Antique Gold

Hauser Dark Green + Avocado Green (1:1)

Primary Yellow + Avocado Green (2:1)

White + Baby Pink Deep (1:1)

Baby Pink Deep + Dark Burgundy (1:1)

White + Antique Mum (3:1) (canvas camouflage)

Antique Mum

Pattern

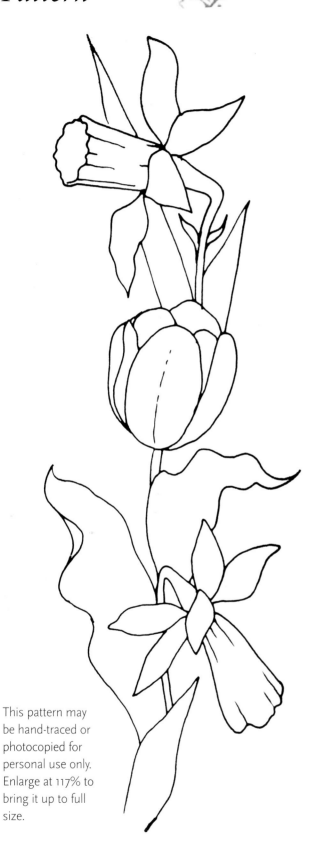

This pattern may be hand-traced or photocopied for personal use only. Enlarge at 117% to bring it up to full size.

Applying Freezer Paper

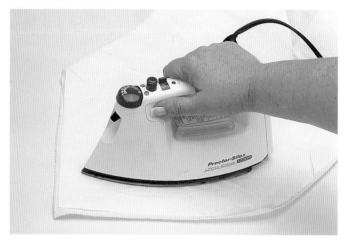

1 I have found freezer paper to be a great help when painting on fabric. It makes the surface sturdier and prevents the paint from bleeding through the work surface.

Cut freezer paper large enough to cover the area you are painting. Iron the paper onto the wrong side (the back side) of the table runner. The steam setting on the iron should be turned off. Freezer paper is plastic on one side and paper on the other. Make sure the shiny side faces the fabric; you will iron on the dull side of the paper. The paper adheres quickly (in only a few seconds) but temporarily to the fabric and peels off easily when you are finished painting. You can find freezer paper next to the aluminum foil in the grocery store.

Hint ~ Instead of using commercial paper palettes, you can use the plastic side of freezer paper as a palette. It's more economical.

Tulip Leaf

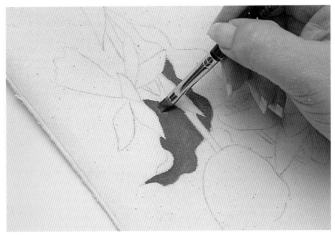

2 Once the freezer paper is in place, transfer the pattern to the fabric using tracing paper and graphite paper. Alternate the directions of the flower patterns around the table runner.

Begin by painting a small area at a time. SoSoft Fabric Paints stay wet longer than regular acrylics do, allowing you to work wet-into-wet in order to blend colors easily. This table runner is large, so working on one small section at a time will prevent you from putting your arm in an area that hasn't dried yet.

Basecoat the tulip leaf (the ruffled leaf) using Avocado Green on a no. 6 shader.

3 To shade the leaves, use Hauser Dark Green with a no. 4 shader. Blend these colors together (you're not floating here). Both colors are wet, so a little wiping with your brush, where the colors meet, will blend the paint smoothly.

4 Use your no. 0 spotter and Hauser Light Green to highlight the leaves.

5 Still using the no. 0 spotter on the edges of the highlights, mix a little bit of Pineapple in with the Hauser Light Green.

Daffodil Leaf and Stems

6 Paint the daffodil leaf (straight leaf) with the no. 0 spotter and Hauser Light Green.

7 Still using the same brush, accent the tips of the leaves with Pineapple.

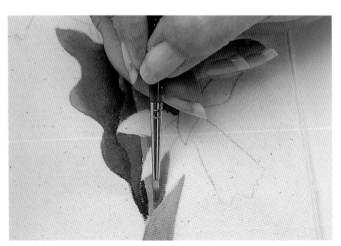

8 With the no. 0 spotter, shade the daffodil leaves using Hauser Dark Green and Avocado Green (1:1).

9 Basecoat the stems with Hauser Light Green. Then highlight with Pineapple, using a no. 4 liner.

10 Shade the stem with Hauser Dark Green, using your no. 4 liner. The tulip and daffodil stems are painted exactly the same way.

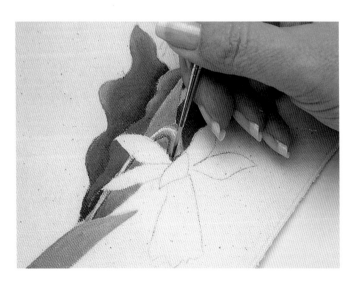

Daffodil

11 Basecoat the daffodil petals with a no. 4 shader and Primary Yellow. Use the no. 0 spotter to shade with Antique Gold, blending it into the yellow.

12 Highlight the daffodil petals with the no. 0 spotter and Pineapple.

13 Use the no. 6 shader to basecoat the trumpet with Pineapple. Mix Primary Yellow and Avocado Green (2:1), and use the no. 0 spotter to shade the trumpet.

14 Using the same brush and White, accent the trumpet.

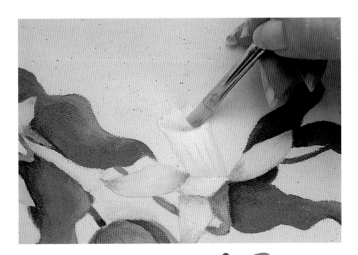

15 With a no. 6 shader, shade the inside of the open trumpet with a float of the Primary Yellow and Avocado Green mixture (2:1) from step 13.

Tulip

16 Use a no. 6 shader and Baby Pink Deep to basecoat the tulip. Sketch in the outlines of the petals with a pencil; the paint will still be wet, but that's okay.

17 Use a no. 0 spotter to shade the tulip with a mix of Baby Pink Deep and Dark Burgundy (1:1). Blend this out into the base color.

18 Load a no. 4 liner with Dark Burgundy and add deeper detail lines.

Final Touches

19 Add highlights to the petals with a mixture of White and Baby Pink Deep (1:1) on a no. 6 shader.

20 Using the same mixture with a no. 0 spotter, add final highlights to the edges of the petals.

As careful as we try to be, goofs can still happen. If you get paint on the canvas where you don't want it, quickly wipe it up without smearing. Scrub the spot with a soft toothbrush and warm soapy water before the paint dries. If this doesn't remove the stain, try to paint over it. I have found that a 3:1 mix of White and Antique Mum matches the color of natural muslin canvas.

Carefully iron the table runner before use. Turn the runner to the wrong side. Lay a press cloth over the fabric and press with a dry iron—as cool as possible. Too much heat can damage the artwork.

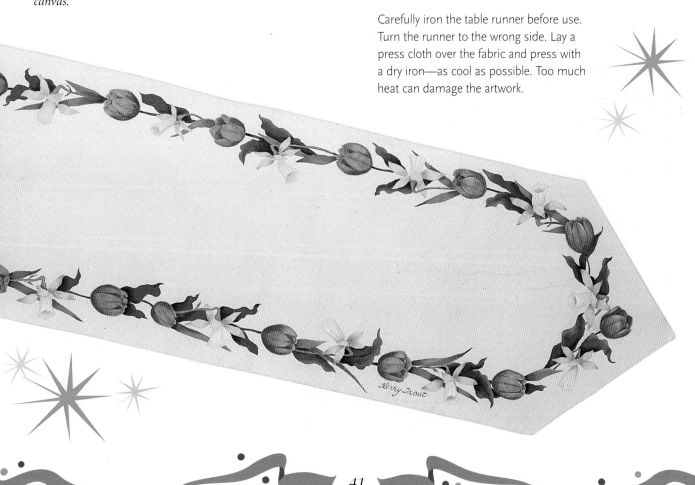

Girl's Birthday
Bugs & Bees Outfit

*A*ny little girl would love to sport this pretty summer T-shirt and matching visor. They're quick and easy to paint, and the pearlescent fabric paint makes them bright and feminine. You could add to this charming ensemble by painting a pair of new white sneakers.

MATERIALS

Loew-Cornell Fabric Painting Brushes
Series 223 no. 4 shader
Series 225 no. 0 round

Additional Supplies
freezer paper
stiff paper or card stock
pencil or disappearing fabric marking pen

Surface
White T-shirt and visor from a department or craft store

Paint
DecoArt SoSoft Shimmering Pearls

Magenta

Christmas Red

Soft Peach

Golden Yellow

White

Grey Sky

White + Grape Purple (2:1)

Grape Purple

Charcoal

Patterns

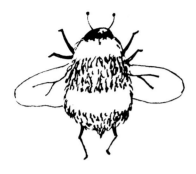

These full-size patterns may be hand-traced or photocopied for personal use only.

Ladybugs

Pre-wash the t-shirt to remove any sizing. Do not use fabric softener.

Lay the shirt flat, front side up. Cut freezer paper the size of the T-shirt and slip it into the shirt, plastic side up. Iron the paper in place. Cut a small piece and iron it onto the inside of the right sleeve.

Transfer the patterns of the ladybugs and bumblebees onto card stock or a suitable heavy paper. I found that, in this case, it's better to trace around the bugs rather than use transfer paper. So place the bug patterns where you'd like them on the shirt and trace around them with either a soft pencil or a disappearing fabric marking pen. I suggest staggering the patterns and angling the directions in which the bees and ladybugs are facing.

🐞 *Three colors are used for the ladybug bodies: Magenta, Soft Peach and lavender (which is a 2:1 mix of White and Grape Purple).*

1 With a no. 4 shader, paint the ladybug's body with Soft Peach. Use the same brush to float Christmas Red onto one side of the body, and then float a thinner area on the opposite side of the body. Paint the head Charcoal with a no. 0 round.

🐞 *Since the fabric paint stays wet longer, you can paint wet-into-wet for easy blending. You'll find it is best to work on only a couple of ladybugs at a time*

2 Add eyes to the head with the same brush. Rinse the brush and pick up Christmas Red to stroke in the line between the wings and to outline the body with a thin line.

🐞 *Use Christmas Red to outline the Soft Peach and Magenta ladybug bodies, and Grape Purple for the ladybug with the lavender body*

3 With the no. 0 round and Charcoal, add legs, antennae and dots (two or more dots as shown). Add two dots in Christmas Red to the antennae. Put two White dots on the eyes.

Bumblebees

1 Use a no. 4 shader to apply Golden Yellow to the body, and to apply White to the wings.

2 Use the same brush to apply Charcoal to the other stripes. Overlap the yellow stripes just slightly by dry-brushing a fuzzy outline around the charcoal stripes. There should be no hard lines between the stripes. For the stripe on the tail end of the bee, make the strokes point toward the tail and make a tiny point with the corner of your brush.

3 Switch to a no. o round, and still using Charcoal, paint the head. The neck area should be drybrushed into the yellow, with a small separation in the yellow stripe made with a stroke of Charcoal. Use the same brush to add the legs and antennae, with little dots on the ends of the antennae. Outline and detail the wings with a no. o round and Grey Sky.

Make little trails of White dip-dots behind the bugs. (Dip-dots are made by dipping the end of your brush handle into the paint and stamping it onto the surface.)

Refer to the labels on each bottle of fabric paint for specific instructions for application, care and maintenance of your painted fabric.

45

Boy's Birthday Dinosaur Desk Set

*E*very little boy loves dinosaurs. Here's a cool desk set you can paint with your choice of dinosaur: a Brontosaurus, a Tyrannosaurus Rex or a Pterodactyl. Paint the tin to hold crayons, markers, collector cards or whatever a little boy treasures. You can even paint a mouse pad to complete the set. Be creative—mix and match dinosaurs and backgrounds on each surface.

MATERIALS

Loew-Cornell Brushes
Series 7300 no. 6 flat shader
Series 7000 no. 2 round
Series 7350 no. 2 liner

Additional Supplies
small scruffy brush
1-inch (25mm) foam brush
DecoArt Americana Spray
  Sealer (DAS 13: matte)
medium sea sponge
tracing paper
graphite paper

Surface
Tin bucket with lid from a craft store
Mouse pad from an office supply store

Paint
DecoArt Americana Acrylics, DecoArt No-Prep Metal Paints (MP)

Shale Green + Black Green (2:1)

Soft Sage

Shale Green

Light Buttermilk

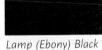
Desert Sand

Lamp (Ebony) Black

Avocado

Black Green

Buttermilk

Sedona Clay (MP)

Bright Yellow (MP)

Artichoke Green (MP)

Khaki Tan

Dark Chocolate

Patterns

This pattern may be hand-traced or photocopied for personal use only. Enlarge at 117% to bring it up to full size.

Tyrannosaurus Rex

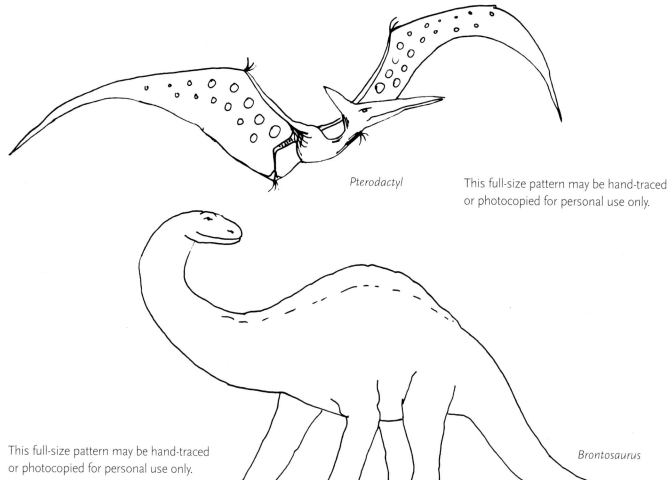

Pterodactyl

This full-size pattern may be hand-traced or photocopied for personal use only.

This full-size pattern may be hand-traced or photocopied for personal use only.

Brontosaurus

Tyrannosaurus Rex

1 With a 1-inch (25mm) foam brush, basecoat the sky with Sedona Clay, gradating down to Bright Yellow. Basecoat the ground with Artichoke Green.

2 Transfer the dinosaur pattern onto the surface using tracing paper and graphite paper. Basecoat the dinosaur with Khaki Tan, using your no. 6 shader. Float Dark Chocolate shading around the edges, using the same brush. Use your small scruffy to stipple Desert Sand onto the rounded areas of the body. Use your no. 2 round and very thin Desert Sand to apply subtle stripes and wrinkles.

3 Use the no. 2 round and Dark Chocolate to apply more stripes and wrinkles. Load Lamp (Ebony) Black on a no. 2 liner to outline and enhance the stripes and wrinkles. With the same brush, add a few teeth with Light Buttermilk. If you want to stroke in a few background trees, use a no. 2 round with Artichoke Green.

Your flat shader is a versatile brush. For basecoating, use the full width of the brush for a smooth, ridge-free finish. However, you can also turn the bristles sideways or at an angle for a narrower stroke. And for an even thinner line, you can use the fine chisel edge—straight up and down (such as the shading under the dinosaurs). Once you learn how versatile your shaders are, you'll be switching brushes less often!

Foliage and Cast Shadows

Paint the surrounding foliage on the mouse pad in Black Green, sponged on with a medium sea sponge. Then pounce on a few branches over that in Avocado. Add just a touch of Shale Green for highlights on the branches. Scatter some foliage in the foreground by painting in some long blades of grass and leafy plants, using your no. 2 liner and Avocado.

Paint a cast shadow under the dinosaur by adding just a touch of Black Green to Avocado to darken the Avocado slightly. Brush this onto the ground, using the no. 6 shader at a sideways angle; holding the brush at this angle makes your strokes thin. Add a bit more Black Green to your brush, and deepen the shadows under the feet and tail, where they meet the ground.

Pterodactyl

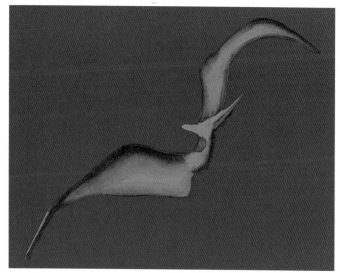

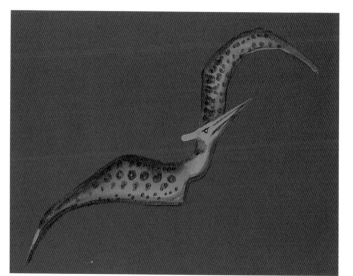

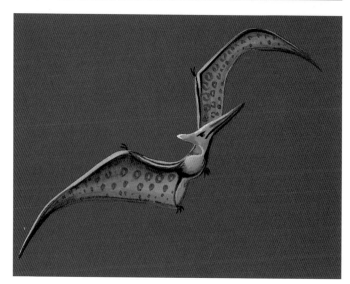

1 Paint the background as you did for the Tyrannosaurus Rex, then transfer the pattern onto the surface. Basecoat the Pterodactyl with Khaki Tan, using a no. 6 shader. With the same brush, float shading around the edges with Dark Chocolate.

2 Use a no. 2 round and thinned Dark Chocolate to apply details to the wings and head.

3 Still using the same brush, highlight the upper edges with Buttermilk. Use Lamp (Ebony) Black to add more details where needed and to paint the feet and eyes.

Brontosaurus

1 Paint the background as you did for the Tyrannosaurus Rex. Using a no. 6 shader, basecoat the Brontosaurus with Shale Green. Use the same brush to contour, by floating a 2:1 mixture of Shale Green and Black Green.

Brontosaurus, continued

2 With a no. 6 shader, drybrush in a highlight of Soft Sage; stroke horizontally across the legs. Deepen the shadows with floats of Black Green.

3 With a no. 6 shader, drybrush strokes of a mix of Shale Green with just a touch of Black Green across the legs and around the neck and tail. Use a no. 2 round to stroke on a few wrinkles at the shoulder with the same mix. Add more highlights with drybrushed Buttermilk. Outline the body with a no. 2 liner and Black Green; also add the nose, eye and mouth.

Add shadows under the Brontosaurus (see Foliage and Cast Shadows on page 49).

Spray the bucket and mouse pad with two coats of matte sealer to protect the painting.

Mother's Day Pillow

These white cotton pillows, with little bouquets of nasturtiums and forget-me-nots, are so delicate and feminine. What mom wouldn't love them? They're fun to paint with the SoSoft fabric paints that allow for easy blending (see page 35 for more information on these fabric paints). You can even personalize the pillow with your mother's initial to make it a very special gift. This elegant yet simple design can be painted in an afternoon, but it will be treasured for generations.

MATERIALS

Loew-Cornell Brushes

Series 7350 no. 1 liner
Series 7300 no. 4 shader
Series 7000 no. 1 round

Additional Supplies

black felt-tip marker
freezer paper
water-erasable fabric marker
 (available in the sewing notions department of your local
 craft store)
iron
tracing paper
straight pins
scissors

Surface

Lace pillow cover from
 Jan Brooks Exclusives

Paint

DecoArt SoSoft Fabric Paints

Primary Yellow

Cadmium Orange

Hauser Light Green

Hauser Dark Green

Primary Blue

White

Hauser Light Green + White (1:1)

Primary Yellow + Cadmium Orange (1:1)

Primary Yellow + White (1:1)

Cadmium Orange + White (1:1)

Terra Cotta

Primary Blue + White (2:1)

Hauser Light Green + Hauser Dark Green (1:1)

53

Patterns

These full-size patterns may be hand-traced or photocopied for personal use only.

Transferring the Pattern

Before you start, you will need to transfer the pattern to the fabric.

Here is the best way to do this when you are working with light-colored fabric.

* Transfer the pattern onto tracing paper with a black felt-tip marker.
* Cut around the pattern and position it inside the pillow cover so that it shows through the fabric. Pin the pattern in the center through the fabric (from the outside) to secure the pattern onto the inside of the pillow cover.
* Cut a sheet of freezer paper the size of the pillow and slip it inside the cover, shiny side toward the front and against the cut out patterns. Place the iron inside of the cover and iron the paper into place.
* The pattern will now be secured in place so you can remove the pins from the front of the pillow.
* Using a fabric marker, trace the pattern lines you see through the fabric.

The freezer paper will prevent the paint from bleeding through to the back of the pillow.

Nasturtiums and Forget-me-nots

1 Using your no. 4 shader, basecoat the orange flowers with a 1:1 mix of Cadmium Orange and White. Basecoat the yellow flowers with a 1:1 mix of Primary Yellow and White.

Basecoat the leaves and all other greenery (stems and calyxes) with Hauser Light Green, using the no. 4 shader.

2 Still using your no. 4 shader, highlight each flower by adding a little more white to it's base color. Then highlight the widest areas of each petal.

Using your no. 1 liner, shade the orange flower with Cadmium Orange applied near the center; use outward strokes. Define the edges of the petals as well. (Shade the base of the buds in the same way.)

Shade the yellow flower in the same manner, using Primary Yellow with a touch of Cadmium Orange added to darken it slightly.

Shade the leaves with Hauser Dark Green; begin at the base and blend outward with the no. 4 shader. Use the no. 1 liner to add a few dark lines coming out from the center of each leaf to its edge. Dab a bit more shading in at the bases of the leaves. Also dab a little of the green into the flower centers as shown.

With a mixture of Primary Blue and White (2:1), dot on little clusters of forget-me-nots, using your no. 1 round.

Add a bit more White to the light blue mixture, and add more little forget-me-not petals around and on the darker petals.

Nasturtiums & Forget-me-nots, continued

3 Use a no. 1 liner with Terra Cotta to add very thin center veins to the petals of the orange flower. Also add a little bit of this around the edge of some of the petals. On the bud, use this color to deepen the shading near the base of the petal at the calyx. Use the no. 1 round to pounce a few dots of Hauser Light Green into the center; add a few dots of Primary Yellow, then a few dots of White.

Paint the center vein of the yellow flower with a thin line of Primary Yellow and Cadmium Orange (1:1). Add a few strokes of Cadmium Orange on the base of the yellow petals near the center. Paint the centers as instructed for the orange flower.

Add a couple of long dotted stamens to both centers with a mix of Hauser Light Green and Hauser Dark Green (1:1). With this same mix, add thin veins to the leaves.

4 With the no. 4 shader and White, drybrush a few highlights onto the flower petals. With the no. 1 round, apply Hauser Light Green to the flower centers and stroke outward to form small stamens (do not cover the darker green base). Apply Hauser Dark Green, heavier this time, to the shaded parts of the greenery.

Dot the centers of the forget-me-nots with a 1:1 mix of Primary Yellow and Cadmium Orange. Add a couple more forget-me-nots on top of the nasturtium petals, as shown. Add leaves to the forget-me-nots, using the no. 1 round with Hauser Light Green and Hauser Dark Green (you may want to loosely mix the different green colors for variation in the leaf colors).

On the large leaf, paint a thin border along the front edge with Hauser Light Green to suggest an upturned edge.

Lettering

If you have a computer, choose a font that you like and enlarge it to the size you want. Or use a copier to enlarge it to the size needed for your particular pillow. Also, you can buy lettering stencils at a craft store, and trace them onto your pillow with a water-erasable fabric marker.

1 Mix up a 1:1 blend of Hauser Light Green and White. Use this mixture to basecoat the letter, using a no. 4 shader for the wide parts, switching to a no. 1 round for thinner areas of the letter.

2 Add a bit more White to the light green mix, and apply this to the widest parts of the letter. Rinse the brush and blend the edges of this lighter color into the paint already applied. With the no. 1 round, paint a 1:1 mixture of Hauser Light Green and Hauser Dark Green into the thinnest parts of the letter.

3 Enhance the letter with forget-me-nots by following the painting instructions on page 55.

When the paint is completely dry, dab the blue marks from the fabric marker with a clean damp cloth to make them disappear. Use a cool iron and a press cloth if you need to press the pillow cover.

Father's Day Dresser Box

Men like small keepsake boxes as much as women do, and this is a handsome box that any dad would be proud to own. It is small enough to fit on his desk or dresser, where he can stash anything from playing cards to pencils to pocket change.

This is an easy project, and a great gift for a birthday or Father's Day. Or you can even do what I'll do with mine—give it to him just because you love him.

MATERIALS

Loew-Cornell Brushes

Series 7300 nos. 6 and 10 shaders

Series 7000 no. 1 round

Series 7350 no. 2 liner

Series 1176 1-inch (25mm) goat hair

Additional Supplies

DecoArt Americana Spray Sealer (DAS 13: matte)

DecoArt Weathered Wood Crackling Medium

DuraClear Satin Varnish

DecoArt Gel Stain (Oak)

small scruffy brush

twig

fine grit sandpaper

tracing paper

graphite paper

soft lint-free cloth

Surface

Lidded keepsake box from Walnut Hollow

Paint

DecoArt Americana Acrylics

Salem Blue

Desert Turquoise

Green Mist

Deep Teal

Titanium (Snow) White

Shale Green

Buttermilk

Soft Black

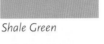
Wisteria + Titanium (Snow) White (1:1)

Black Green

Milk Chocolate

Neutral Grey

Deep Teal + Black Green (2:1)

Wisteria

Milk Chocolate + Titanium (Snow) White (2:1)

Pattern

This full-size pattern may be hand-traced or photocopied for personal use only.

Basecoating and Crackling

Sand the wood, then seal the box with a matte spray sealer.

Basecoat around the sides with Buttermilk. Then apply the crackling medium according to label directions.

Topcoat with Shale Green; as the paint dries, it will crackle. (For step-by-step crackling information, see page 121.)

Landscape

Blend Desert Turquoise downward

Blend White upward

Blend Deep Teal upward

Add the mountains

Add grass with thinned paint

1 Using a no. 10 shader, paint the sky, starting at the top with Desert Turquoise, gradating to the horizon with Salem Blue. Add a bit of Titanium (Snow) White and blend this up into the Salem Blue.

2 Paint in the mountains, using your no. 6 shader with a 1:1 mixture of Wisteria and Titanium (Snow) White.

3 With a no. 2 liner and varied blends of thinned Deep Teal and Green Mist, add strokes of grass. Always stroke from the ground up when painting grass.

Trees

1 Stipple in the trees with a small scruffy brush. First pounce on a 2:1 mix of Deep Teal and Black Green in a triangle shape, with a heavier concentration of color toward the middle.

☙ *How to Stipple ~ Stippling is often used for painting trees and foliage. Dampen your scruffy brush and wipe dry. Dip it into full strength paint, then blot it on a paper towel. Pounce the brush up and down on the surface and it will make irregular blotches of color.*

2 Rinse the brush. Now stipple just Deep Teal onto the tree, with a heavier concentration of the color on the left side of the tree.

3 Rinse the brush once more and stipple Green Mist onto the left side of the tree. Add a shadow on the ground under the tree and on the right side of the tree, using the chisel edge of your no. 6 shader and diluted Deep Teal.

Twig Letters

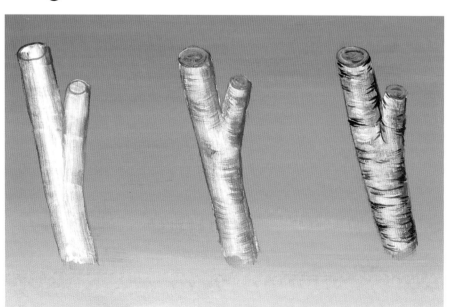

1 Use graphite paper and tracing paper to trace on the lettering pattern. Basecoat the twig letters with two coats of Titanium (Snow) White. Using a no. 6 shader, float (see page 10) Neutral Grey on each edge of the twig.

2 Use your no. 1 round to paint the cut ends of the twig with a 2:1 mixture of Milk Chocolate and Titanium (Snow) White. With Neutral Grey on a no. 6 shader, drybrush (see page 11) the bark in random places from the edge inward. Arch the stroke slightly to show a rounded shape.

3 Use thinned Soft Black on a no. 1 round to add detail to the bark.

Finishing Touches

Float Black Green around the edges of the box sides. When dry, apply one coat of a satin varnish. Then antique with an oak-color gel stain, following the manufacturer's directions on the label. Use a 1-inch (25mm) goat hair brush to apply the stain, working on a small section at a time. With a soft lint-free cloth (cotton T-shirt material is ideal), wipe off the excess stain. If there was any crackling once the varnish dried, this will now become apparent. When the box has thoroughly dried, seal it with a matte spray sealer to protect the painting.

Finish the inside of the box in any way you desire.

For a unique touch, cut a twig about 1-½ inches (32mm) long, paint it as you did the birchbark twig letters, then glue it to the front of the box as a handle.

PROJECT 8

June Wedding

White coral bells
upon a slender stalk,

Lilies of the valley
deck my garden walk.

Oh, don't you wish that
you could hear them ring!

That will happen only
when the fairies sing.

— *Author unknown*

Whenever I see lily of the valley, I think of this old song, which is what inspired me to use this delicate flower to embellish these pieces. What could more sweetly symbolize wedding bells? Your gift to the bride and groom will be unique—there's no chance of duplicating a wedding gift when you present the happy couple with this matching set, lovingly painted by you.

MATERIALS

Loew-Cornell Brushes

Series 7300 nos. 4 , 6 and 10/0 shaders

Series 7350 no. 1 and 10/0 liners

Additional Supplies

DecoArt Americana Spray Sealer (DAS 13: matte)

sea sponge

latex gloves

low-tack painter's tape

pencil

tracing paper

graphite paper

waxed paper

Magic Rub® eraser

pen or stylus

Surface

Heart-shaped porcelain box from J.C.'s Pour 'N More

Wooden picture frame from a craft store

Paint

DecoArt Americana Acrylics

Taffy Cream

Light Buttermilk

French Vanilla

Golden Straw

Olive Green

Hauser Medium Green

Plantation Pine

Delane's Deep Shadow

Light Mocha

Eggshell

Titanium (Snow) White

Light Mocha + Eggshell (1:1)

Light Buttermilk + Olive Green (2:1)

Huaser Medium Green + Olive Green (1:1)

Golden Straw + Delane's Deep Shadow (2:1)

Pattern

This pattern may be hand-traced or photo-copied for personal use only. Enlarge at 125% percent to bring up to full size.

Undercoat

1 Seal the surface with a matte spray sealer. If you're painting the wooden picture frame, apply a matte spray sealer to the entire frame (remove the glass first).

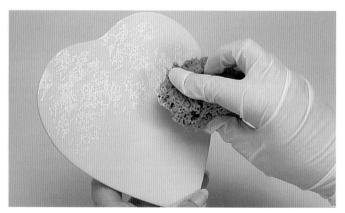

2 Use a small sea sponge to sponge diluted Taffy Cream (dilute with water) onto both the top and bottom of the porcelain box. Allow to dry. You may want to wear latex gloves to protect your manicure.

If you're painting the frame, basecoat the entire surface with two coats of a 1:1 mix of Light Mocha and Eggshell. Let dry between coats.

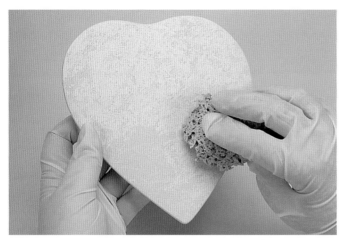

3 Using the same sponge, apply diluted French Vanilla over the Taffy Cream. Allow to dry.

4 Now sponge diluted Golden Straw over the French Vanilla. On the lid, add a heavier concentration of color on the lower-left side of the heart. Before the paint dries, go over the entire surface with a clean damp sponge to blend and soften the paint. Allow to thoroughly dry. Spray the surface once again with sealer; this will make the surface a little smoother, creating an easier surface on which to paint the flowers.

5 Place the lid back on the box and sponge diluted Hauser Medium Green on the lower-left side of the top. Sponge this on lightly, then go back with the clean side of the sponge to blend and soften it even more.

6 Carry the green over the bottom sides and the lid as shown.

Transfer Pattern and Paint Leaves

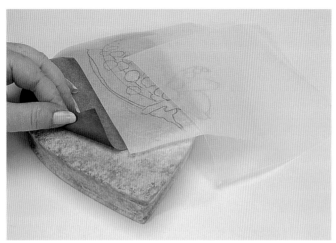

7 Transfer the pattern to the top of the lid. You will need three items for transferring the pattern: graphite paper, the traced pattern and waxed paper (see page 10).

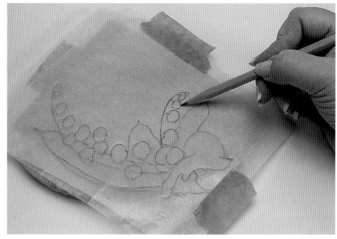

8 Use low-tack painter's tape to attach the graphite paper to the back of the pattern. Then lay the pattern and graphite paper (graphite side down) onto the lid and tape them to the surface. Tape the waxed paper on top of the pattern. The waxed paper helps to save the pattern from overuse. Also, as you trace the pattern, you can see the white marks in the wax, which ensures that you have not missed any pattern lines.

9 Basecoat the leaves and grass with Olive Green (the light value of green), using a no. 6 shader. You'll need two coats. Be sure to paint over the pattern lines, and let the paint dry between coats. If you're painting the frame, just follow these same step-by-step directions for the flowers, stems and leaves.

10 Using the same brush with Hauser Medium Green (the middle value of green), darken the areas shown. While the paint is still wet, add a touch of Olive Green to your brush, blending the greens together where they meet.

11 Still using the no. 6 shader, add Plantation Pine (the darkest value of green) to the leaves. Plantation Pine is transparent, so in the deepest shadows you will need to add a second coat. You may be covering up the area where the bloom patterns are, but that's okay. If you prefer, you can choose to paint around them.

12 Highlight the leaves with a 2:1 mix of Light Buttermilk and Olive Green. Add highlights to the edges of the leaves and damp blend (see page 14).

13 Load a no. 1 liner with Hauser Medium Green, and paint the area where stems overlap the background. Paint the area where the stem overlaps the leaf with Olive Green. Highlight the darker stem at the top with the same brush and Olive Green. You can add touches of Olive Green wherever you want.

Blossoms

14 Basecoat each blossom with Light Buttermilk, using a no. 4 shader. Use a 10/0 shader to paint the buds; they will need two coats.

15 Look at the pattern and use a pencil to lightly sketch in the openings on the blossoms. You want to show which direction each blossom faces.

16 Mix Light Buttermilk and Olive Green (2:1), and shade the bells, using a 10/0 shader.

17 Load a 10/0 liner with a mixture of Hauser Medium Green and Olive Green (1:1), and add deeper shading to the bells.

18 Use a no. 4 shader to float Hauser Medium Green on the inside of the bell openings.

19 Load a no. 1 liner with Olive Green, and add stems to the bells. Use Titanium (Snow) White on a 10/0 shader to highlight the left side of the bells.

20 Highlight the closed buds with Light Buttermilk on a 10/0 shader. Use a 10/0 liner with DeLane's Deep Shadow to paint the stamens. Still using the 10/0 liner, highlight the stamens with a 2:1 mix of Golden Straw and DeLane's Deep Shadow.

When the paint has thoroughly dried, erase any pencil marks with a Magic Rub® eraser. Then seal with two light coats of a matte spray sealer to protect the paint. Insert clean glass into the frame.

4th of July
Americana Picnic Set

*W*e love to fill our summers with barbecues, parties and lots of outdoor dining. Many of these will take place over holiday weekends.

Give your summer holiday table a patriotic theme with these quick and easy red, white and blue painted accessories: a wooden utensil caddy, serving tray and matching candles.

Since I like the vintage look, I used a crackling and an antiquing medium to give some "intant aging" to the tray and caddy. But feel free to leave them as they are—just use your artistic license and personalize them in any way you wish.

MATERIALS

Loew-Cornell Brushes

Series 7000 no. 2 round
Series 7300 no. 10 shader
Series 1176 1-inch (25mm) goat hair

Additional Supplies

DecoArt Weathered Wood Crackling Medium • DuraClear Satin Varnish • DecoArt Gel Stains (Oak) • DecoArt Americana Spray Sealer (DAS 13: matte) • compressed sponge • 1-inch (25mm) foam brush • raffia or ribbon • pencil • ruler • chalk pencil • low-tack painter's tape • fine grit sand-paper • soft cloth • tracing paper • white graphite paper

Surface

9x12-inch (23x30cm) wooden tray from a craft store • Citronella candles from a dis-count store • Utensil caddy from Country Craft Coop

Paint

DecoArt Americana Acrylics, DecoArt Dazzling Metallics (DM), DecoArt No-Prep Metal Paint (MP)

Napa Red

Desert Sand

Deep Midnight Blue

Milk Chocolate

Glorious Gold (DM)

Ivory (MP)

Patterns

This full-size pattern may be hand-traced
or photocopied for personal use only.

Utensil Caddy

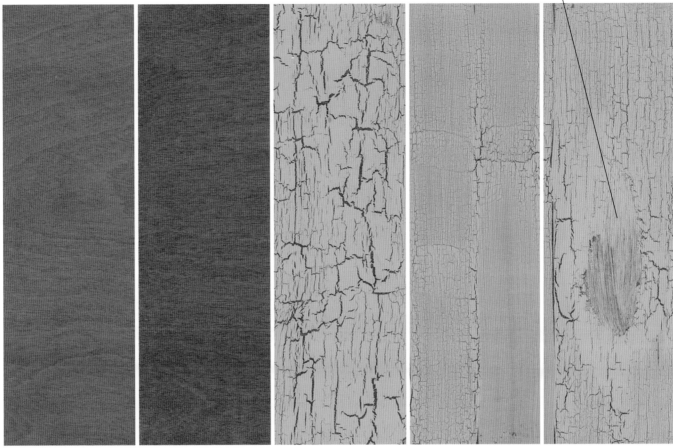

You may have to apply two coats of the crackling medium. The wood should be shiny before you start.

Large cracks— Desert Sand is applied thick—undiluted.

Very small cracks— Desert Sand, diluted with water, is applied in a thin coat.

Oops! This is what happens when you go over a stroke!

1 Sand the caddy with fine grit sandpaper. Using the 1-inch (25mm) foam brush, stain the outside with an oak gel stain. (Important: do not seal wood that you intend to stain.)

2 Starting ½-inch (12mm) from the end (at the seam), use a pencil to mark off 1⅝-inch (41mm) stripes on each side.

3 If you have not used a crackling medium before, practice on cardboard or scrap wood first. With a 1-inch (25mm) foam brush, apply crackle medium to the sides, ends, inside of the end pieces and the tops of the inner sections. Let dry according to label instructions (approximately 45 minutes).

4 Using a no. 10 shader, paint the red stripes with Napa Red and the white stripes with Desert Sand. Paint each stripe with one stroke. Do not restroke (see oops! above).

5 Let the stripes dry completely, then coat with a satin varnish. Allow to dry.

6 With a 1-inch (25mm) foam brush, paint the ends of the caddy with Deep Midnight Blue. Let dry completely, then transfer the star pattern to the ends. Apply crackle medium again on the inside of the star. Let dry. Use the same brush to apply Desert Sand over the crackle. Paint the handle with Glorious Gold on a 1-inch (25mm) foam brush.

7 Float Milk Chocolate around the stars and around the stripes with a no. 10 shader. When dry, coat with a satin varnish. Allow to dry. Now you are ready for antiquing.

To antique, apply oak gel stain with a 1-inch (25mm) goat hair brush to small areas at a time. Wipe immediately with a soft cloth.Rub gently, using circular motions to remove the excess stain. The stain will enhance the crackling. Let dry again. Spray with a matte sealer to make the wood moisture-resistant and to protect the painting.

Antiquing adds mellow aging to surfaces.

Tray

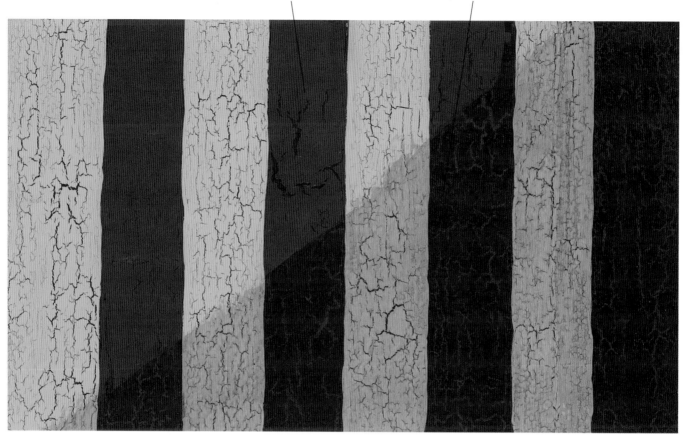

Let the stripes dry completely, then apply a satin varnish.

Coat with a satin varnish before antiquing. Apply antiquing and wipe off with a soft cloth.

1 Sand and stain the tray as instructed in step 1 on page 75. When it's completely dry, use a chalk pencil to mark off a blue field for the stars, 4⅞-inches (12cm) x 5⅝-inches (14cm), in the top left corner. Apply crackling medium, as directed on the label, to the tray surface.

2 Now tape off the stripes of the flag. Apply a strip of 1-inch (25mm) low-tack painter's tape (purple or blue tape) first across the top of the tray surface (right against the edge). Apply a second strip across the bottom of the tray surface. Then find the center of the tray, and place a third strip of tape across the center. Finally, center the last two strips between the center strip and the edge strips.

Burnish (rub) the edges of the tape well, so paint won't seep beneath the edges.

3 Use a no. 10 shader to paint the exposed stripes with Desert Sand (remember to apply the paint with one stroke), and remove the tape before the paint dries completely. Using the same brush, paint the remaining stripes with Napa Red. Paint the field with Deep Midnight Blue.

4 Once the blue field dries, draw a 3-inch (7.6cm) circle for a guide (use a chalk pencil). Then use tracing paper and white graphite paper to transfer eight small star patterns around the circle.

5 Use a no. 2 round to paint the stars with Desert Sand. Paint the inside of the tray frame with Desert Sand, using a 1-inch (25mm) foam brush. Paint the outside of the frame with Deep Midnight Blue using a no. 10 shader. With the same brush, paint the edges with Glorious Gold. Still using the no. 10 shader, float Milk Chocolate around the stars and around the stripes.

6 Apply a satin varnish. When it's dry, antique the tray following the instructions for antiquing shown in step 7 on page 75.

Star-spangled Candles

These citronella candles came in little red, white and blue metal buckets. As summer approaches, look around your local craft and home stores for all sorts of candles and holders, which are great for lighting up picnic tables and backyard barbecues. Use the primitive star patterns on page 74 to cut out a star from a compressed sponge. Place the sponge in a glass of clean water and watch it expand to full size. Squeeze out the sponge until it's just damp. Load the sponge with Ivory metal paint and sponge stars in a random pattern onto the metal buckets. Let the paint dry completely, then protect it with several coats of a matte spray sealer. If you like, tie a bow of raffia or ribbon around the rim for a country accent.

Applying a spray sealer to all your painted surfaces will help prevent food stains from ruining your Americana picnic set.

Summer Garden Vegetable Bucket

*M*y grandma used to take a tomato basket to the garden when picking vegetables for supper. It was sturdy and held a lot of produce; however, those old baskets are no longer around.

I have a unique and even better suggestion for the avid gardeners on your gift list! Paint this handy vegetable bucket for them to use on their daily trips to the garden. They will think of you while using it to gather their harvest.

MATERIALS

Loew-Cornell Brushes

Series 7000 no. 1, round

Series 7300 nos. 4 and 10 shaders

Series 7350 no. 1 liner

Additional Supplies

DecoArt Gel Stain (Oak)

DecoArt Perfect Crackle

DecoArt Americana Spray Sealer (DAS 13: matte)

1-inch (25mm) bristle brush

1-inch (25mm) foam brush

tracing paper

graphite paper

soft cloth

compressed sponge

homespun fabric (optional)

Surface

Galvanized no. 8 bucket from any home improvement store

Paint

DecoArt Americana Acrylics, DecoArt No-Prep Metal Paint(MP)

Hauser Light Green + Titanium (Snow) White (1:1)

Plantation Pine

Avocado

Hauser Light Green

Georgia Clay

Khaki Tan

Titanium (Snow) White

French Grey Blue

Black Plum

Napa Red

Cranberry Wine

Cadmium Yellow

Cadmium Orange

Napthol Red

Antique Lace (MP)

Avocado + Hauser Light Green (1:1)

Avocado + Hauser Light Green (1:3)

Avocado + Plantation Pine (1:1)

Cadmium Orange + Cadmium Yellow (1:1)

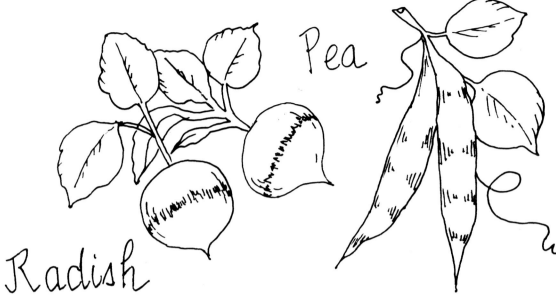

This pattern may be hand-traced or photocopied for personal use only. Enlarge at 133% to bring it up to full size.

This full-size pattern may be hand-traced or photocopied for personal use only.

First Steps

Basecoat the bucket with Antique Lace metal paint, using a 1-inch (25mm) foam brush.

Cut ½-inch (12mm) squares from a compressed sponge. Dip into Khaki Tan, and add a checked trim around the top edge.

Use tracing paper and graphite paper to transfer the patterns onto the bucket. (Paint the radish and pea leaves by following the leaf directions on page 29.)

Radishes and Peas

1 Use the no. 4 shader, and basecoat the radishes with Titanium (Snow) White tinged with a hint of Cranberry Wine and French Grey Blue. Paint the red half of the radish by applying Cranberry Wine, starting at the stem and lifting the brush halfway down the radish. Leave a ragged edge by using a drybrush technique at this edge. The Cranberry Wine may need two coats. Let dry.

2 Using the same brush, float Black Plum around the red area only.

3 Still using the same no. 4 shader, float French Grey Blue around the edges of the lower half of the radish. Using the same brush, highlight the radish with dry-brushed strokes of Titanium (Snow) White.

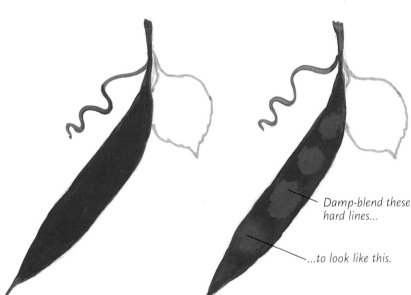 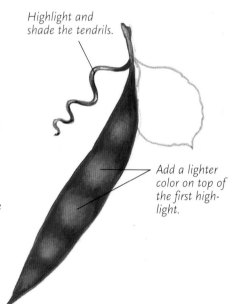

Damp-blend these hard lines...

...to look like this.

Highlight and shade the tendrils.

Add a lighter color on top of the first highlight.

1 Using the no. 4 shader, basecoat the pea pods with Avocado. Shade with a mix of Avocado and Plantation Pine (1:1).

Use the no. 1 liner brush and thinned Avocado to draw out a thin, curly tendril.

2 Using the same brush, highlight with a mix of Avocado and Hauser Light Green (1:1).

Damp-blend (see page 14) into the base color to soften any hard edges.

3 Still using the no. 4 shader, highlight again with a lighter mix of Avocado and Hauser Light Green (1:3) drybrushed (see page 11) onto the first highlight, just in the centers.

Shade with a mix of Avocado and Plantation Pine (1:1). Use the same highlight mixture to add accents to the tendrils.

Tomatoes

1 Using the no. 10 shader, undercoat the tomato with Cadmium Orange and let dry. Paint over the stem and leaves that are on the front of the tomato. It's easier to paint over them than to paint around them. The stem and leaves can be added later.

Still using the no. 10 shader, basecoat with two coats of Napthol Red. Use the same brush to apply Georgia Clay around the outer edges and in the creases for shadow. Then deepen the shadows on the lower right with Napa Red.

2 Use your no. 4 shader to paint the leaves and stem with Avocado. Shade with Plantation Pine. Use the no. 1 round to highlight the leaves with Hauser Light Green and Titanium (Snow) White (1:1).

Use your no. 1 round to apply Napa Red onto the tomato, just under the leaves. This will simulate a cast shadow.

3 When dry, use your no. 10 shader to apply a thin coat of a mix of Cadmium Orange and Cadmium Yellow (1:1) to the left side of the tomato. Using the no. 4 shader, dab a few thinned Titanium (Snow) White highlights onto the tomato and leaves.

Finishing Touches

Apply step 1 of DecoArt Perfect Crackle, with a 1-inch (25mm) bristle brush, all over the bucket. (Follow label directions.) When dry, apply step 2 and allow to dry and crackle completely. Wait several hours before antiquing.

To antique, apply oak gel stain, with a 1-inch (25mm) bristle brush, to small areas at a time, wiping immediately with a soft cloth. Use circular motions to remove the stain, rubbing gently. The stain will remain in the cracks as you wipe off the excess.

Let dry again, and spray with a matte spray sealer to make the bucket moisture-resistant.

Use strips of homespun to wrap the handle and to make bows.

New Baby Butterfly Lamp

*Y*ou are sure to brighten up a nursery with the colorful butterflies on this easy-to-paint baby lamp.

These little lamps are so inexpensive that you can afford to keep one on hand for those last-minute gift dilemmas. And they are so easy, you could even paint one the night before! It's sure to be the most popular gift at the baby shower.

MATERIALS

Loew-Cornell Brushes
Series 7300 no. 6 flat shader
Series 7530 no. 10/0 liner
Series 7000 no. 1 round

Additional Supplies
pencil
craft knife
card stock or heavy paper

Surface
Small white lamp from Linens 'n Things

Paint
DecoArt Americana Acrylics

Boysenberry Pink

Baby Pink

Pink Chiffon

Titanium (Snow) White

Olive Green

Winter Blue

Taffy Cream

Wild Orchid

Instead of using graphite paper, I found it easier to cut out the butterfly patterns (making them into stencils) and to trace them onto the lamp shade.

Transfer the patterns onto card stock or a heavy paper. Carefully cut out the butterflies with your craft knife, but don't try to cut the antennae. Now your patterns have become stencils.

It's always helpful to work out a design on paper first, before applying it to the lamp. Place the stencil onto the lamp or lampshade and carefully trace around it with a very light pencil mark. Do this with all the stencils. You may choose to paint

just the lampshade or just the base. It will look great any way you choose.

Use your imagination to come up with your own look, and make sure you save your cutout patterns for future projects.

You can follow the painting directions for the butterflies shown or feel free to change the colors for each pattern to create your own personal look.

For best results when using a craft knife, use a fresh blade. Slip a piece of wood or commercial cutting board under the paper to protect your table. Also, wear safety glasses.

Patterns

These patterns may be hand-traced or photocopied for personal use only. Enlarge at 133% to bring them up to full size.

Yellow Butterfly

1 Use your no. 6 shader to basecoat the center of the wings, on the yellow butterfly, with Taffy Cream and the ends of the wings with Olive Green.

2 Using the same brush, float Olive Green to soften the area where the Taffy Cream center and Olive Green ends meet.

Helpful Hint ~ Take care when outlining and painting the antennae. Thin the paint as little as possible. Paint that is too thin is likely to bleed into the lampshade's fabric.

3 Still using your no. 6 shader, add a few strokes of Titanium (Snow) White on the base of the wing (next to the body), stroking outward from the center. Float Baby Pink onto the tips of the wings with your no. 6 shader. Dab some oblong dots onto the green sections with your no. 1 round. Outline the wings with your 10/0 liner and Olive Green. With the same brush and paint, add antennae (see helpful hint). Paint the body with Wild Orchid, using your no. 1 round. Highlight the body with a thin line of Titanium (Snow) White.

Blue Butterfly

1 Basecoat the top wings of the blue butterfly with Winter Blue. The bottom wings are Winter Blue, with a touch of Titanium (Snow) White added. Using your no. 1 round, apply Titanium (Snow) White to the base of the wings, then pull the stroke outward into the wing.

2 Use your no. 6 shader to float Wild Orchid along the wing edges.

3 Use the 10/0 liner to outline the wings with Wild Orchid and to add the antennae. With your no. 1 round, paint the body Boysenberry Pink.

Pink Butterfly

1 Using your no. 6 shader, basecoat the wings of the pink butterfly with Pink Chiffon. Use your no. 1 round to apply Baby Pink to the base of the wings, then pull the stroke outward into the wing. Don't go as far as the center of the wing. Damp-blend (see page 14), if necessary, to smooth the transition between the colors. Allow to dry, then pencil in the wing designs.

2 With your no. 6 shader, float Boysenberry Pink around the wing edges; keep the float thinner around the bottom wings.

3 Using your no. 1 round, paint the wing designs with Winter Blue and float Wild Orchid onto the outer edges. Using the same brush, paint the body Olive Green and highlight with Titanium (Snow) White. Use your 10/0 liner to outline the wings with Boysenberry Pink and to add the antennae. Finish by outlining the wing designs with Baby Pink.

QUICK PROJECT 12

Autumn *Applefest Linens*

*F*abric painting is making a big resurgence, and isn't always limited to plain fabrics.

Look how these apples give a refreshing kick to homespun table linens. This is a wonderful project that looks great when used indoors or out. Paint a set for an autumn house warming gift or for a wedding shower.

MATERIALS

Loew-Cornell Fabric Bristle Brushes

Series 223 nos. 6 and 8 flat shaders

Series 228 no. 1 round

Additional Supplies

white graphite paper

freezer paper

iron

tracing paper

toothpick

Surface

Green homespun table topper

Coordinating napkins and potholder from Jan Brooks Exclusives

Paint

DecoArt SoSoft Fabric Paints

Hauser Light Green

Hauser Dark Green

White

Burnt Sienna

White + Buttermilk (1:1)

Hauser Light Green+White (1:1)

Dark Chocolate

Christmas Red

Alizarin Crimson

Antique Mum

Primary Yellow + White (1:1)

Buttermilk

Primary Yellow

Antique Gold

Patterns

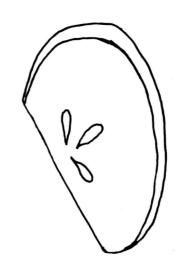

These full-size patterns may be hand-traced or photocopied for personal use only.

Preparation

Wash and dry the linens; do not use fabric softener. Place some freezer paper, plastic side down, against the wrong side of the fabric, right behind the area where your design will be applied (see page 36). Using the dry setting on your iron, iron the freezer paper to the fabric. Freezer paper will seal the back of the fabric and mini-

mize bleed-through of paint, while also giving stability to the fabric.

Turn the fabric over and transfer the pattern onto the fabric, using white graphite paper and tracing paper. You will not need to apply freezer paper to the potholder.

Table Topper and Potholder

1 Unless otherwise indicated, use the no. 8 shader for the entire project. Undercoat the leaves and apples with Hauser Dark Green; this will prevent the print from showing through the painted design. (If you are not using this particular green patterned fabric, you may not have to undercoat. Test your fabric to see if this is needed.)

When the undercoat is dry, basecoat the apples with one coat of Antique Gold; let dry. The Antique Gold will help brighten the red of the apples. Paint the apples Christmas Red, with a band of Alizarin Crimson around the outer edge about ½-inch (12mm) wide. While the paints are still wet, blend the colors slightly to soften the hard line between the two reds. Reds are often transparent, so you'll want to apply two coats of each red, making sure that the paint dries completely between coats.

Basecoat the leaves and stems with Hauser Light Green.

2 When the reds are dry, apply a very light coating of Primary Yellow to the midsection of the apple. The stroke direction should curve with the contour of the apple. Blend out any hard lines. Use the no. 6 shader to apply Hauser Light Green to the dimple where the stem emerges. Also, bring a few strokes outward and down the side of the apple. Drybrush Hauser Dark Green onto the lower edges of the leaves. Keep the direction of the strokes in mind—move from the outside edge to the center vein, with a slightly arched slant. Apply the same color to the upper side of the center vein, making the same type of strokes, but from the center outward. Use the no. 1 round to paint the stem Burnt Sienna; highlight with White while it's still wet.

3 Mix a tint of Hauser Light Green and White (1:1). Drybrush this onto the leaves with the no. 6 shader for highlights. Use your no. 1 round to highlight the small stem, and paint a thin line down the center of the leaves. Apply Primary Yellow, again, with the no. 6 shader on the roundest part of the apple. Use very light, feathery strokes. When dry, apply very light strokes of highlight with White. Add a final highlight to the stem with White, using your no. 1 round.

Blossoms and Apple Slices

1 Undercoat the leaves, blossoms and buds with White, using the no. 8 shader. When dry, use the same brush to basecoat the leaves and stems with Hauser Light Green.

2 Recoat the blossom and bud with White. Use your no. 1 round to apply strokes of Primary Yellow into the center of the flower, then stroke outward. Use the no. 6 shader to apply Hauser Dark Green down the center of the leaf and on the opposite edge. Drybrush the same color outward at an angle from the center, then inward at an angle from the outer edge to suggest veining.

3 Use a toothpick to dot Hauser Dark Green into the center of the flower. Use your no. 1 round to add more visible veins to the leaves. Shade the bottom edge of the stem with Hauser Dark Green. Mix Hauser Light Green and White (1:1), and drybrush this on the leaves for highlights. Use the toothpick, also, to dot Hauser Light Green in the center.

4 Add more White to the Hauser Light Green mixture used in step 3, and use a toothpick to add a few dots of this lighter mixture to the center of the flower. Add a little Primary Yellow to the base of the bud. Use your no. 1 round to add sepals to the bud with Hauser Light Green. Shade at the base with Hauser Dark Green. Highlight the stem and sepals with the final leaf highlight color.

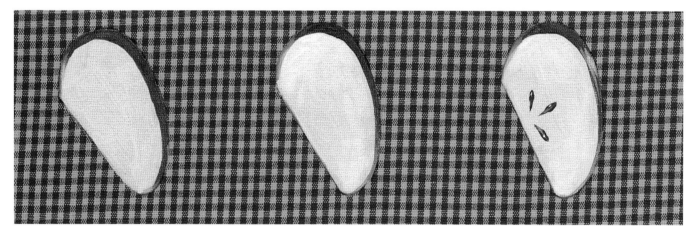

1 Iron a 4-inch (10cm) section of freezer paper onto the wrong side of the corner of the napkin. Transfer the pattern. Undercoat the apple slice, using the no. 6 shader and Antique Mum. This prevents the pattern of the fabric from showing through. When dry, basecoat with a mix of White and Buttermilk (1:1). Use your no. 1 round to apply two coats of Christmas Red to the right side of the slice. Apply a few strokes of Hauser Light Green to the corners of the slice on the left side. Apply a second coat of the White and Buttermilk mixture to the slice. Let dry.

2 Apply Alizarin Crimson to the upper part of the skin with your no. 1 round. Mix Primary Yellow and White (1:1), and use the round brush to paint three comma strokes on the middle of the apple slice. These are the seed hulls.

3 With the no. 1 round, paint three comma strokes for seeds using Dark Chocolate. Highlight by touching in tiny dots of White. Also apply a few strokes of White for highlight on the red skin.

Follow the paint manufacturer's instructions for care and laundering of your painted linens.

Silver & Golden Anniversary
Memory Albums

Silver and golden wedding anniversaries are wonderful milestones to celebrate. What could be more meaningful to a couple than to present them with a photo album or scrapbook of their many years together? Inspired by a 1940s wedding card, this album is sure to be a gift they'll treasure.

Make the album extra special by painting a beautiful personalized cover. You could even fill the album with photos taken at the anniversary party.

If you cannot find an album that does not have a design on it, that's okay; just paint over the design.

The following steps are for the silver album. For the golden album, see page 107.

SILVER ANNIVERSARY MATERIALS

Loew-Cornell Brushes

Series 7300 nos. 10/0, 4, 6, 10 and 12 shaders

Series 7350 no. 1 liner

Series 7051 no. 1 script liner

Additional Supplies

1-inch (25mm) foam brush or basecoater • sea sponge • latex gloves • DecoArt Brush 'n Blend Extender • craft knife • DecoArt Pearlizing Medium • DecoArt Americana Spray Sealer (DAS 13: matte) • graphite paper • tracing paper • low-tack painter's tape • toothpick • pencil • paper towels • straightedge • hair dryer • gesso

Surface

Vinyl picture album from a craft or office supply store

Paint

DecoArt Americana Acrylics, DecoArt Dazzling Metallics (DM)

Boysenberry Pink + Titanium (Snow) White (1:1)

Cool White

Shimmering Silver (DM)

Blue Chiffon

Titanium (Snow) White

Winter Blue

Williamsburg Blue

Light French Blue

Williamsburg Blue + Shimmering Silver (DM) (1:1)

Hauser Medium Green

Yellow Ochre

Hauser Medium Green + Yellow Ochre (1:1)

Boysenberry Pink

Uniform Blue

Boysenberry Pink + Titanium (Snow) White (1:2)

Patterns

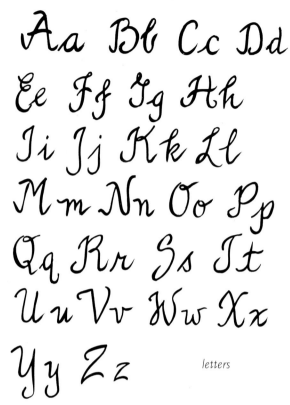

letters

This pattern may be hand-traced or photocopied for personal use only. Enlarge at 204% to bring it up to full size.

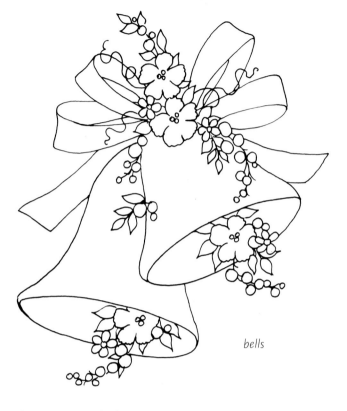

bells

This pattern may be hand-traced or photocopied for personal use only. Enlarge at 153% to bring it up to full size.

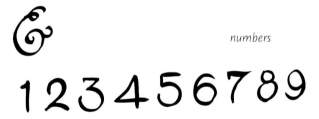

numbers

This pattern may be hand-traced or photocopied for personal use only. Enlarge at 117% to bring it up to full size.

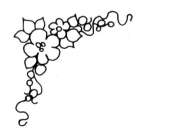

flowers

This pattern may be hand-traced or photocopied for personal use only. Enlarge at 212% to bring it up to full size.

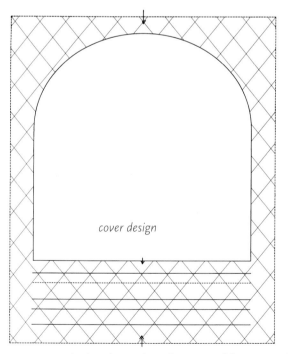

cover design

This pattern may be hand-traced or photocopied for personal use only. Enlarge at 270% to bring it up to full size.

Basecoating

1 If your album cover is printed, undercoat it with gesso. Then, use your 1-inch (25mm) foam brush or basecoater to basecoat the photo album with two coats of Blue Chiffon. Thin Cool White with water, and using the sea sponge, sponge on top of the Blue Chiffon. (Use latex gloves to protect your manicure.)

2 Without rinsing the sponge, dip it into the Blue Chiffon, and go over the previous sponging to soften the white a bit. Allow to dry, then sponge on undiluted pearlizing medium.

3 A hair dryer provides a quick and handy way to dry the paint between steps.

Trellis Border

4 When the paint is completely dry, transfer the trellis border pattern. Enlarge the trellis pattern to fit the album you are painting; cut out the pattern on the dotted line. Place the pattern on top of graphite paper, and use a straightedge to follow the pattern lines. If the graphite gets smeared on the album surface, use Brush 'n Blend to remove it.

5 Use low-tack painter's tape to tape off a border all the way around and about ⅛-inch (3mm) in from the outside edges of the album cover. Also tape off the back and the inside edges so you have a neat margin. Miter the corner; use the craft knife to cut the tape from the outside corner (where the tape is crossed) to the inside corner as pictured. Be careful not to cut into the surface of the album.

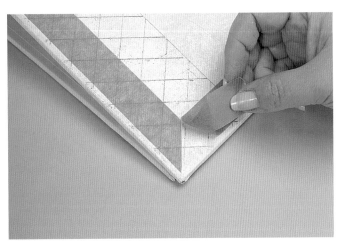

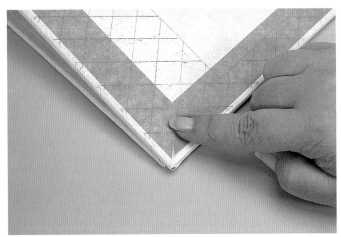

6 Pull the tape up and remove the cut-off ends. You will pull up the two excess ends; just discard them.

7 Press the corners back down together. Use your fingers to smooth the tape all the way around.

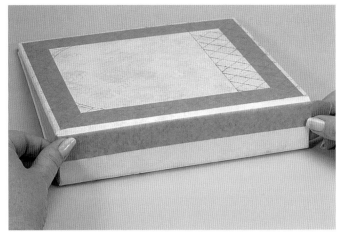

8 Also tape off the spine of the binder; just fold the ends underneath for neatness.

9 Place something like a roll of tape between the album covers while you are painting, so the edges don't touch each other. Use Shimmering Silver and your no. 10 shader to paint the border. You will need two coats; allow to dry between coats. When dry, remove the tape.

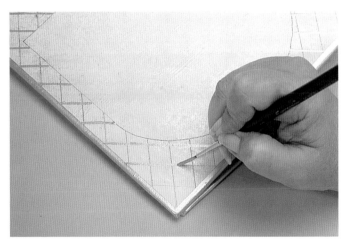

10 Use your no. 1 script liner to paint the trellis. Thin Shimmering Silver with water, just enough for the paint to flow properly. If the paint is thinned too much it becomes transparent and won't cover the pattern lines. The inner border of the trellis design needs to be a little bit wider than the outer border.

11 Once the paint has thoroughly dried, clean off any excess graphite marks using a little Brush 'n Blend on a paper towel.

Ribbon

12 Since you'll be replacing the pattern several times throughout this project, you'll need to make registration marks so that it can be realigned easily. Simply use a pencil to mark the pattern and the album, so that you can later realign the marks. Use graphite paper to transfer the pattern onto the album. Transfer the bow, the bells and the flowers around the perimeter. Don't transfer the flowers that are in the foreground yet; the bells have to be painted first.

13 Basecoat the ribbon with Winter Blue, using your no. 6 shader. You will need two coats.

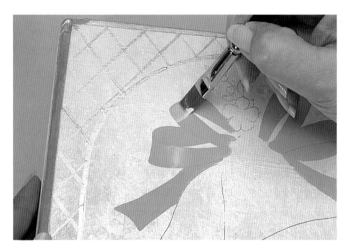

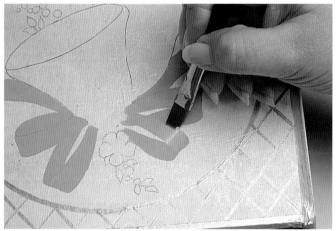

14 After the paint is dry, use a pencil to resketch the ribbon edges. With your no. 10 shader, add highlights to the ribbon with a double float (see page 11) of Blue Chiffon. Load the brush and stroke in the float across the ribbon.

15 Flip the brush and stroke the float right next to the other float so the lines meet. You may find it helpful to turn your work instead of trying to stroke in the opposite direction. The important thing is to make the stroke comfortable for you.

16 Still using the no. 10 shader, float Williamsburg Blue into the inside of the loops.

17 Using the same brush and paint, float some shading where the ribbon casts a shadow.

18 Switch to the no. 1 liner and lighten the top edge of the ribbon with Blue Chiffon.

Bells

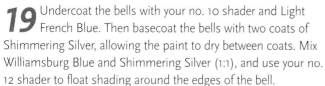

19 Undercoat the bells with your no. 10 shader and Light French Blue. Then basecoat the bells with two coats of Shimmering Silver, allowing the paint to dry between coats. Mix Williamsburg Blue and Shimmering Silver (1:1), and use your no. 12 shader to float shading around the edges of the bell.

20 Mix a touch of Titanium (Snow) White with Shimmering Silver, and use your no. 6 shader to drybrush highlighting onto the bell as shown. This gives the bell more dimension.

21 Using the registration marks, realign the pattern and trace on the edges of the bells and the bell openings. Use the no. 1 script liner to outline the bells with Williamsburg Blue. With the same brush, add highlights to the silver using Titanium (Snow) White. Allow to dry.

Flowers

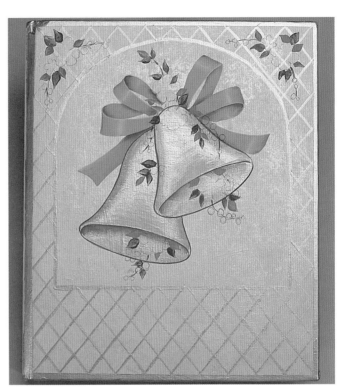

22 Replace and realign the pattern once again, and transfer the foreground flowers onto the album cover. At this point, you can erase the registration marks. Also transfer the flower patterns to the two corners of the cover. With your no. 4 shader and Hauser Medium Green, paint the stems and small stroke leaves (see page 12).

23 Use Hauser Medium Green and Yellow Ochre (1:1) on the same brush to paint the remaining stroke leaves.

24 Undercoat the large flowers with Titanium (Snow) White, using the no. 4 shader. Double load your no. 10 shader with Williamsburg Blue and Titanium (Snow) White, and stroke in each petal. Wiggle the brush as you stroke to get a ruffled petal (see page 15).

Berries

25 Using the no. 10/0 shader, undercoat the berries with Titanium (Snow) White. Using the same brush with Boysenberry Pink, paint the darker berries. The darker berries may require two coats.

26 Add Titanium (Snow) White to the Boysenberry Pink (1:1), and use your no. 10/0 shader to paint the light pink berries. Use this mixture and the same brush to highlight the darker berries. Highlight the light pink berries with Boysenberry Pink and Titanium (Snow) White (1:2).

27 Use a toothpick with Titanium (Snow) White to dot the brightest highlight onto each berry highlight. Use Titanium (Snow) White with your no. 4 shader to stroke in the little five petal flowers. Dot in the flower centers on the white flowers using Yellow Ochre on the end of the brush. Also dot in the blue flower centers, using a (1:1) mixture of Hauser Medium Green with Yellow Ochre.

28 Use slightly thinned Titanium (Snow) White and your no. 1 script liner to add some tendrils (see page 13).

Lettering

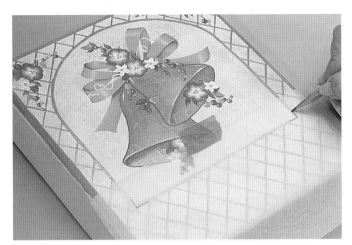

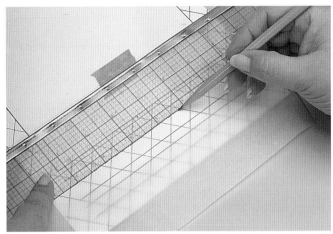

29 Now it's time to personalize your album. Getting the lettering straight is important, so follow these steps carefully. Cover the area with a half sheet of tracing paper, and tape it down with low-tack painter's tape. Since you'll be replacing this tracing paper, make registration marks as you did in step 12. Make two marks on the lower corners of the arch and two more at the bottom corners of the album.

30 Now take the tracing paper and move it onto the original pattern, lining up the marks to center it. Trace the lettering lines off the original pattern, including the centering marks. Always use a straightedge to transfer straight lines.

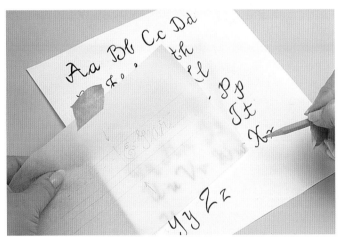

31 Spell out the names and dates that you want. Count all characters and spaces (a character is any letter, number or punctuation mark). Count the letter "I" and each comma as one half character. Now divide the total by two to find the center. The center may not be a letter—it may even be a space. Begin at the center and trace each character onto the tracing paper.

32 Line up the tracing paper with the registration marks, and use graphite paper to transfer the lettering onto the album.

33 Use your no. 1 liner and Uniform Blue to paint the letters.

Protect the album with two coats of matte spray sealer.

Golden Anniversary Album

The directions for the golden anniversary album are the same as the Silver Anniversary album, except for the colors.

1 Cover any preprinted designs with gesso. Use your 1-inch (25mm) foam brush or basecoater to basecoat the album with Taffy Cream. Sponge on Buttermilk, followed by pearlizing medium. Let dry.

2 Transfer the trellis pattern, then tape off the border. Paint the border with your no. 10 shader and Glorious Gold; you may need two coats. Remove the tape. Use your no. 1 liner and two coats of Glorious Gold to paint the lines of the trellis.

3 Replace (realign) the pattern and transfer the bells and bow. Use your no. 6 shader to paint the bow Moon Yellow. Float True Ochre to shade, and double float Light Buttermilk onto the rounded parts of the ribbon.

4 Undercoat the bells with True Ochre. Basecoat the bells with two coats of Glorious Gold. Let dry completely.

5 Replace (realign) the pattern and trace on the bell openings and the flowers.

6 Highlight the bells, using your no. 12 shader and Champagne Gold. Then using the same brush, shade by floating a mixture of Glorious Gold and Asphaltum (1:1) onto the edges of the bells, and below the front outer rim (on the inside). Use your no. 1 liner to stroke on more Champagne Gold highlights. Outline the bells with the shade mixture and your no. 1 script liner.

7 Use your no. 4 shader to paint the stems and leaves with random mixes of Hauser Medium Green and Light Buttermilk.

8 Undercoat the large flowers and the berries that overlap the bells with Titanium (Snow) White.

9 Use your no. 1 liner to apply small white blooms. Use your no. 10 shader, double-loaded with True Ochre and Titanium (Snow) White, to wiggle petals onto the large flowers. Mix Hauser Medium Green and Yellow Ochre (1:1), and with the end of your brush, dot in centers.

10 Apply True Ochre centers to the white blooms.

11 Using the 10/0 shader, paint berries randomly, alternating Summer Lilac and Wild Orchid. Mix in one part Titanium (Snow) White to lighten each, and highlight the left side. Dot with Titanium (Snow) White.

12 Follow steps 29 through 33 for lettering, but instead of the Uniform Blue used in step 33, use your no. 1 liner and a mixture of Glorious Gold and Asphaltum (1:1).

GOLDEN ANNIVERSARY MATERIALS

Loew-Cornell Brushes

Series 7300 nos. 10/0, 4, 6, 10 and 12 shaders

Series 7350 no. 1 liner

Series 7051 no. 1 script liner

Additional Supplies

1-inch (25mm) foam brush or basecoater • sea sponge • latex gloves • DecoArt Brush 'n Blend Extender • craft knife • DecoArt Pearlizing Medium • DecoArt Americana Spray Sealer (DAS 13: matte) • graphite paper • tracing paper • ow-tack painter's tape • toothpick • pencil • paper towels • straightedge • hair dryer • gesso

Surface

Vinyl picture album

Paint

DecoArt Americana Acrylics, Dazzling Metallics (DM)

Summer Lilac

Wild Orchid

Hauser Medium Green + Yellow Ochre 1:1

Hauser Medium Green

Glorious Gold (DM) + Asphaltum 1:1

Asphaltum

Champagne Gold (DM)

Glorious Gold (DM)

Titanium (Snow) White

Light Buttermilk

Taffy Cream

True Ochre

Yellow Ochre

Buttermilk

Moon Yellow

QUICK PROJECT 14

Halloween Scarecrow

*H*ere's a fun fall painting idea for your porch. I painted this scarecrow on an old ironing board. He'll be right at home amid your pumpkins, gourds or Indian corn decorations.

The brush sizes for this project will depend on the size of your surface. Please see step 1 for more brush information.

MATERIALS

Loew-Cornell Brushes
Series 7300 nos. 4, 6, 10 and 12 shaders

Series 7051 no. 2 script liner

Series 7520 ½-inch (12mm) filbert rake

Additional Supplies
½-inch (12mm) scruffy shader

1-inch (25mm) flat shader

DecoArt Americana Spray Sealer (DAS 12:gloss)

black permanent marker (optional)

Kerry's Liquid Shadow

Surface
Wooden ironing board from an antique store

Paint
DecoArt Americana Acrylics

Khaki Tan

Red Iron Oxide

Uniform Blue

Lamp (Ebony) Black

Black Forest Green

Jack-O'-Lantern Orange

Cadmium Orange

Tomato Red

Deep Midnight Blue

Antique Maroon

Asphaltum

Georgia Clay

French Grey Blue

Lemon Yellow

Burnt Orange

Napa Red

Milk Chocolate

Marigold

Titanium (Snow) White

Avocado

Dark Pine

French Grey Blue + Titanium (Snow) White (1:3)

Khaki Tan + Titanium (Snow) White (2:1)

Kerry's Liquid Shadow

109

Patterns

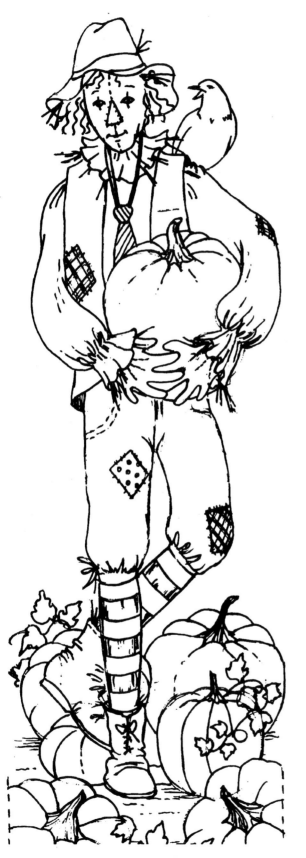

This pattern may be hand-traced or photocopied for personal use only. Enlarge at 142% to bring it up to full size.

This pattern may be hand-traced or photocopied for personal use only. Enlarge at 117% to bring it up to full size.

Basecoating

1 Your first step is to basecoat in all the colors. Instead of telling you what size brush to use for basecoating, I'll just advise you to use the largest brush you can for the area you are painting. This means using the full width of the brush. Go to a smaller brush when the spaces get tight—don't try to paint a small space with the corner of a larger brush. For this project, you will need all the shaders listed in the materials list.

Block in the following colors: Lamp (Ebony) Black for the hat, Uniform Blue for the hatband, Khaki Tan for the head and Lamp (Ebony) Black for the crow. Basecoat the shirt and the dark stripes in the socks with Red Iron Oxide. Basecoat the vest with Dark Pine and the pants with Uniform Blue. The light stripes in the socks are Khaki Tan, the shoes are Milk Chocolate and the ground is Asphaltum. The pumpkins are two different shades of orange, but all the pumpkins are under-coated with Marigold.

Next, basecoat the dark pumpkins with Cadmium Orange; the light pumpkins are basecoated in Jack-O-Lantern Orange. Basecoat the leaves with Avocado. The patches on the scare-crow's pants are plaid, using Napa Red and Dark Pine. The patch on the shirt is Uniform Blue and the patch on the vest is Khaki Tan.

Paint solid, opaque colors for your basecoat rather than the washes you see here (see note below). Some colors, such as the oranges, are going to require more layers, but we'll get to that later.

Note ~ I have used washes rather than opaque basecoats for my demonstration so that I could retain the black lines in the pattern. You will be outlining everything at the end of the project, but I wanted you to continue to see the outlines as I demonstrated the steps for you.

Shading

2 Now you will begin to add shading, starting with the vest. Float shading on the vest using Black Forest Green. Choose the largest brush possible when floating. Float shading onto the shirt using Antique Maroon. You will float shading onto the pants using Deep Midnight Blue. The dark stripes on the socks are Antique Maroon against the Tomato Red. The Khaki Tan stripes on the socks are shaded with Milk Chocolate. The shoes are shaded with floats of Asphaltum. Put another coat of the respective oranges on the pumpkins. Shade around the edges of the lighter pumpkin with floats of Cadmium Orange, then also float it in a striping manner, from the top down, to form the creases in the pumpkins. This will show up especially well on the pumpkin that the scarecrow is holding. On the other pumpkins, these creases will be indicated by black lines. Shade the Cadmium Orange pumpkins in the same manner using Georgia Clay. Basecoat the stems with Khaki Tan. See page 114 for directions for painting the leaves.

Highlighting

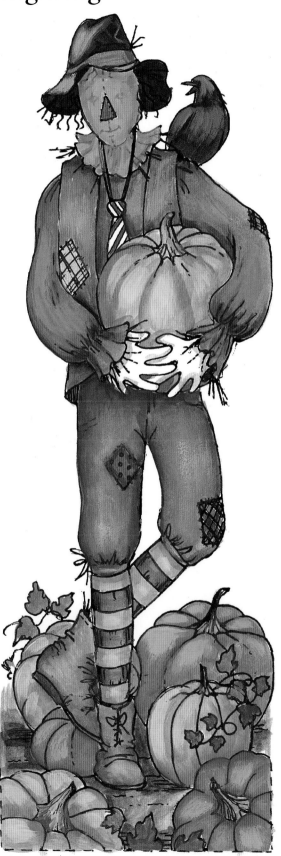

3 Now you will highlight everything, starting with the hat. Mix a bit of Titanium (Snow) White into Lamp (Ebony) Black, and drybrush some gray highlights onto the left side. This will be on the rim and the top-left side. (I will not describe the steps for the face here; I have detailed the face on pages 114 and 115.) Highlight the crow with the same gray mixture that you used to highlight the hat. Use drybrush strokes on the left wing, the breast and the head. Add a bit of Titanium (Snow) White to Dark Pine (just enough to lighten it up a little), and using a ½-inch (12mm) scruffy shader, drybrush this onto the vest. Always be sure to keep the highlighted areas separated from the shaded areas (see techniques, page 14). The basecoat must separate a shaded area and a highlighted area. For example, the vest is basecoated with Dark Pine, shaded with Black Forest Green, highlighted with a lighter mix of green. This lighter mix of green and the Black Forest Green must be separated by the Dark Pine. Gradual transitions from darker values to lighter values on two-dimensional surfaces create the illusion of dimension and contour.

Highlight the shirt in the same way as the hat and vest. Mix a bit of Titanium (Snow) White into Red Iron Oxide and drybrush this highlight onto the fullest part of the sleeve and the large folds of the sleeve. Undercoat the tie and basecoat the gloves with Titanium (Snow) White.

Drybrush French Grey Blue onto the fullest part of the pants to make them appear worn like denim. Add a bit of Titanium (Snow) White to Khaki Tan and add a highlight to the front of the tan stripes on the socks. Also highlight the red stripes by adding a bit of Titanium (Snow) White to Red Iron Oxide. Add a little bit of Khaki Tan to Milk Chocolate and highlight the shoes. Remember that the highlight and the shading on these shoes have to be separated by the Milk Chocolate basecoat.

Let's move on to the pumpkins. Highlight the light pumpkins (the ones basecoated with Jack-O-Lantern Orange) with Lemon Yellow as shown. To highlight the darker (Cadmium Orange) pumpkins, add just a bit of Titanium (Snow) White to some Jack-O-Lantern Orange. Make sure the highlight does not touch the indented areas where the black lines will go. Later, we'll add shading on either side of the black lines to add dimension to each section of the pumpkins. Be sure to leave some basecoat color between the highlights and the areas where the shading will go.

Paint the stripes on the tie with Tomato Red. Shade the gloves with a mix of French Grey Blue and Titanium (Snow) White (1:3).

Leaves Detail

Basecoat the leaves with Avocado.

Float Lemon Yellow against the leaf edges, then outline in Lamp (Ebony) Black and add veins.

Basecoat the leaves with Avocado using the no. 10 shader. Float Lemon Yellow against the leaf edges. Outline in Lamp (Ebony) Black and add veins as shown at left.

Face Detail

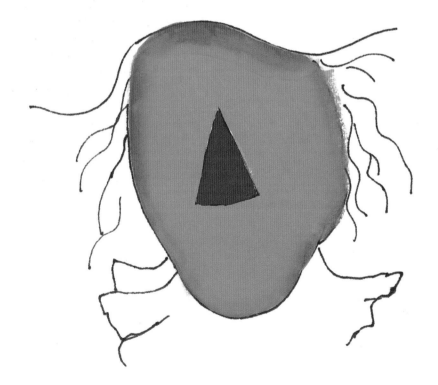

1 Basecoat the scarecrow's face with Khaki Tan. Float Milk Chocolate around the face and into the neck folds with a no. 12 shader. Basecoat the nose with Tomato Red.

Face Detail, Continued

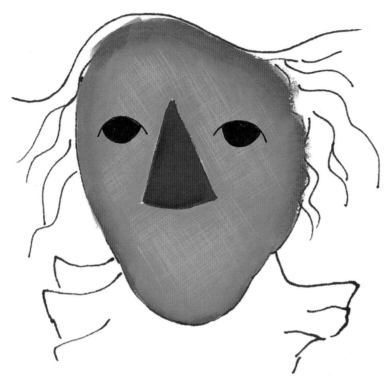

2 Using a ½-inch (12mm) rake brush, apply crosshatch texturing to the face and neck with a mixture of Khaki Tan and Titanium (Snow) White (2:1). Paint in eyes with Lamp (Ebony) Black. Float Napa Red around the left side of the nose.

3 Mix a touch more Titanium (Snow) White into your cross-hatching mixture of Khaki Tan and Titanium (Snow) White (2:1), and add a few more strokes to lighten the cross hatching. Add crosshatched cheeks with thinned Tomato Red. Add finishing details: dot the eyes with Titanium (Snow) White, use Lamp (Ebony) Black to outline the nose with stitch marks and paint on the mouth. Add Liquid Shadow under the hat and chin, then outline in Lamp (Ebony) Black.

Final Shading and Highlighting

For face detail, see pgs. 114 - 115.

For leaf detail, see pg. 114.

4 Add more shading and more highlighting. Mix thinned Titanium (Snow) White with just a touch of Lamp (Ebony) Black to dull the white, and use a rake brush to add rough highlights to the hat and to the bird. Create a tattered look to the the vest, shirt and pants by making very thin crosshatched strokes of the dull, thinned white on the highlighted areas.

Use Marigold and a no. 2 liner brush for the first layer of straw coming out of the scarecrow's collar, sleeves, vest, socks and shoes; also add a few sprigs coming out of the hatband. Make the straw coming out of his hat a little curlier than the rest. Add a little Titanium (Snow) White to the Marigold to lighten it up, and paint another layer of straw over the Marigold layer.

To shade the pumpkins, use Georgia Clay for the darkest areas of the dark pumpkins, then shade the lighter pumpkins with Burnt Orange. Add some Lamp (Ebony) Black to Asphaltum and, with a small brush, darken the area of the ground underneath the pumpkins.

Apply Liquid Shadow to the following areas: underneath the hat to shade the forehead, on the right side of the chin and collar, on the shirt where the vest is shading it, on the gloves where the sleeve casts a shadow, and also on the pumpkin where the scarecrow's hands cast a shadow. Also use Liquid Shadow to intensify the shadow on the pants right underneath the pumpkin, to shade the right side of his legs and shoes, and to add final dark shadows to the pumpkins.

Finally, float Milk Chocolate around the scarecrow, the crow and the pumpkins, using a 1-inch (25mm) shader.

Outlining

When the paint is completely dry, go back in and trace over all of the lines with a black permanent marker or a no. 1 liner loaded with Lamp (Ebony) Black. Be sure to make the straw marks.

After the paint is completely dry, make sure to protect the surface with gloss satin spray sealer.

PROJECT 15

Thanksgiving Tray

Celebrate the beginning of the holiday season with this beautiful Thanksgiving tray. It will fit in easily with the decor of the changing season. You could hang this tray in the dining room or even display it on your mantle.

Paint it in a day for yourself or give it to a special friend or relative who has a November birthday.

MATERIALS

Loew-Cornell Brushes

Series 7000 no. 4 round

Series 7300 nos. 6 and 10 shaders

Series 7350 nos. 10/0 and 1 liners

Series 1176 1-inch (25mm) goat hair

Series 7400 ¼-inch (6mm) and ½-inch (12mm) angular shaders

Additional Supplies

DecoArt Americana Wood Sealer

DecoArt Weathered Wood Crackling Medium

DecoArt Americana Spray Sealer (DAS 13:matte)

DuraClear Satin Varnish

DecoArt Gel Stains (Oak)

DecoArt Brush'n Blend Extender

foam brush

jagged rock

sanding block

gloves

old toothbrush

low-tack painter's tape

tracing paper

graphite paper

soft lint-free cloth

popsicle stick

Surface

Wooden tray from the Stone Bridge Collection

Paint

DecoArt Americana Acrylics, DecoArt Dazzling Metallics (DM)

Georgia Clay

Honey Brown

DeLane's Deep Shadow

Olive Green

Milk Chocolate

Golden Straw

Light Buttermilk

Hauser Medium Green

Brandy Wine

Shading Flesh

Antique Maroon

Tangelo Orange

Burnt Umber

Camel

Glorious Gold (DM)

Camel + Honey Brown (1:2)

Heritage Brick

Bright Yellow

Raw Sienna

Patterns

Golden Straw

Raw Sienna

Honey Brown

Georgia Clay

DeLane's Deep Shadow

Bright Yellow

This pattern may be hand-traced or photocopied for personal use only. Enlarge at 153% to bring it up to full size.

Bright Yellow

This full-size pattern may be hand-traced or photocopied for personal use only.

DeLane's Deep Shadow

Give Thanks

This pattern may be hand-traced or photocopied for personal use only. Enlarge at 142% to bring it up to full size.

Basecoating and Crackling

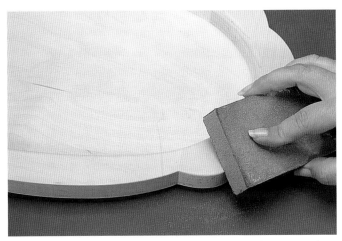

1 Use a sanding block to smooth out any imperfections in the wood.

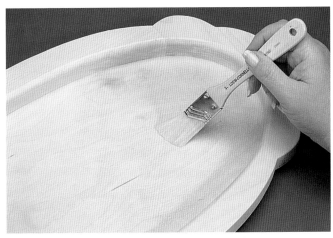

2 Apply a wood sealer to the surface using your 1-inch (25mm) goat hair brush.

3 Basecoat the whole tray with Camel, using a foam brush. The center area will need two coats. Paint the sides with Glorious Gold. Use a 1-inch (25mm) goat hair brush to apply crackling medium over the gold-painted sides. (If you haven't used a crackling medium before, please practice on a similar surface before applying it to the tray.) Allow to dry before proceeding.

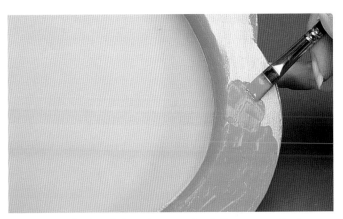

4 Using a flat brush (sized appropriately for your particular surface), apply a thick coat of Honey Brown over the crackling medium on the edges of the tray. As the paint dries, it will crackle and the gold underneath will show through. Allow this to dry thoroughly.

5 Enlarge the patterns to a size that fits the center of your tray, and use graphite paper to trace them onto the surface. You don't need to trace the leaf veins at this time. Make registration marks on the pattern and the surface, as you will be replacing the pattern to trace the veins. Use your no. 6 shader with Light Buttermilk to undercoat the three yellow leaves (the ones labeled Golden Straw, Honey Brown and Bright Yellow on the pattern). These are the only leaves that will need an undercoat. Then basecoat all the leaves according to the colors indicated on the pattern. Use the no. 10 shader for the large leaves. You will need two coats of each color.

Leaves

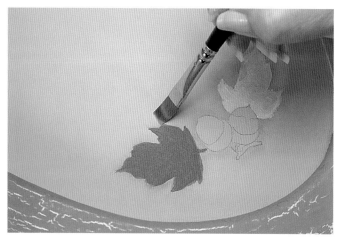

6 Using your no. 10 shader, add shading around the leaves and acorns with a float of Honey Brown.

7 Replace the pattern, using the registration marks to realign it. Trace the primary veins only; you will draw the secondary veins with the brush. Paint the leaves in the background first (the two bright yellow leaves). Load the no. 6 shader with Brush 'n Blend and Light Buttermilk and add this to the middle section of the leaf. Use your 1/2-inch (12mm) angular shader to float Olive Green around the edges of the yellow leaves.

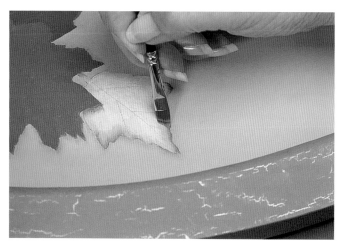

8 After this dries, use your 1/4-inch (6mm) angular shader to float Hauser Medium Green around the tips of the leaves. Also float this color up against the leaf that overlaps this one. Treat this area as a cast shadow.

9 Paint the veins on the yellow leaf with Olive Green using the no. 1 liner. When painting veins, always start your stroke at the base of the leaf and arch the veins slightly.

10 Float Milk Chocolate around the edges of the Honey Brown leaf using your ¼-inch (6mm) angular shader. On the edges that are turned out, use the no. 10/0 liner to stroke on some Golden Straw. Switch to the no. 1 liner and thinned Milk Chocolate to pull out the small veins from the center vein. Remember to arch the veins slightly to keep them natural-looking. Thin some Golden Straw and go over the brown veins with the same brush.

11 On the Golden Straw leaf, use the no. 6 shader and float Olive Green on the tips. Switch to the ¼-inch (6mm) angular shader and add a little Brush 'n Blend, then shade the leaf with Honey Brown where it butts up against the larger, Georgia Clay-basecoated leaf. Thin some Honey Brown and use your no. 1 liner to pull out the veins.

12 Use your no. 6 shader to float Antique Maroon around the edges and along the center of the Georgia Clay leaf.

13 Still using your no. 6 shader, float Hauser Medium Green around the leaf. Apply Brush 'n Blend and add Tangelo Orange to the midsection of each leaf half. Blend this out to meet and blend with the green float.

Leaves, continued

14 Use your no. 1 liner with Antique Maroon to paint in the first layer of veins. Highlight those with very thin Tangelo Orange (the Antique Maroon should still show through slightly) to give the veins dimension. Highlight some of the forks in the veins with Tangelo Orange on the same brush.

15 Use your ½-inch (12mm) angular shader to shade the leaf by floating DeLane's Deep Shadow around the tips and along the center.

16 Apply Brush 'n Blend to your brush, add Shading Flesh, then wipe the Shading Flesh across the leaf.

17 Use Brandy Wine and your no. 1 liner for the veining. Also use your ¼-inch (6mm) angular shader to float a little Hauser Medium Green on the edge of the leaf. Add the highlighting to the veins with your no. 1 liner and thinned Shading Flesh. Remember that the veins go all the way to the edges of the leaves. Use the no. 10/0 liner and Camel, mixed with Honey Brown (1:2), to make some holes in the leaves by dabbing with the tip of the brush.

Holes and Acorns

18 Use your ¼-inch (6mm) shader to paint a cast shadow on the inside of the hole by adding a crescent-shaped shading of Milk Chocolate. Still using your ¼-inch (6mm) liner, float Shading Flesh on one side of the hole. Using the tip of your ¼-inch (6mm) angular shader, float Brandy Wine on the other side of the hole.

Turn your work, when necessary, for more stroke control.

19 Basecoat the acorns using Milk Chocolate on the no. 6 shader. With the chisel edge, add some shading to the stems with Burnt Umber. Still using the same brush, float Burnt Umber around the inside edge of each acorn.

20 Add highlights, using the same brush with Honey Brown; stroke downward and damp-blend around the edges (see page 14).

Acorns and Spattering

21 Using your no. 1 liner, outline the cap of the acorn with Burnt Umber. Also make crisscross marks for texture.

22 Add a little Light Buttermilk highlighting on the acorns with your no. 6 shader, and drybrush a little on the nut. Switch to the no. 1 liner, and add some little highlights on the outside edges.

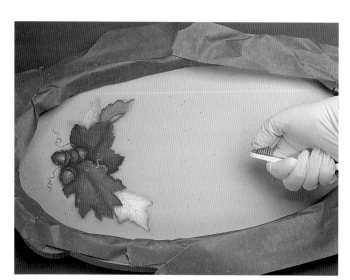

23 With Burnt Umber and your ¼-inch (6mm) angular shader, float in some deeper shading, especially under and around the acorns. You can add this anywhere you think more shading would be effective. You could even darken the float in some places around the leaves for more depth.

Tape the edges of the tray with low-tack painter's tape (see hint below). Use an old toothbrush to spatter thinned Honey Brown over the surface of the tray. Also spatter thinned Milk Chocolate over the same area. Finally, rinse the toothbrush and flick on clear water, to soften the spatters; let some of them bleed together. Allow to thoroughly dry before proceeding.

Hint ~ If your tape is not low-tack, you can press the sticky side onto your clothing, then pull it off to remove some of the adhesive.

24 Remove the tape. Center the lettering pattern and transfer it to the tray surface. Don't let the lettering intimidate you—if you hold your brush just like you do a pencil, you'll be more sure of yourself. Whenever you feel a little unsure, just take some time to practice and you'll quickly become confident with your strokes. Use your no. 4 round to paint the letters with Heritage Brick. Follow the pattern with one stroke. Where the letters are thick, bear down on the brush, where they are thin, lift up on the brush. Use the tip of the brush to paint the serifs.

25 Come around and bear down. A swift, steady hand is required here. If your strokes are shaky, you are painting too slowly.

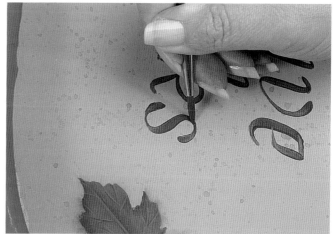

26 On the letters S, G, and V, where the serifs are large, paint the middle of each letter first. Then beginning at the serif, press down, then lift up. These larger serifs are simply comma strokes.

27 Apply less pressure on the brush when you join strokes at the center.

28 Switch to the no. 1 liner and highlight by outlining the right side edges of each letter with Glorious Gold (do not thin the paint).

29 When the paint is thoroughly dry, use a jagged rock to distress the sides of the tray. Roll it across the surface and lightly tap it against the edges. You should have random, natural-looking distress marks.

30 Stir the varnish thoroughly (never shake varnish; this causes bubbles). Use a 1-inch (25mm) goat hair brush to apply the varnish to the entire tray; then allow to dry. (Note: Be aware that certain conditions may affect the varnish as it dries. I painted my tray in an air-conditioned room, and to my delight, the varnish crackled somewhat. This effect can also be achieved by placing the varnished item in front of a fan.)

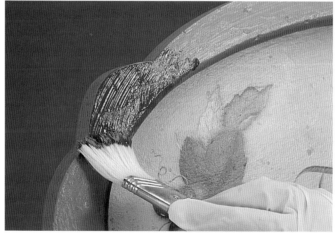

31 Antique the tray by applying oak gel stain, using the 1-inch (25mm) goat hair brush; work on one small section at a time.

Final Steps

32 With a soft lint-free cloth (T-shirt material is ideal), wipe off the excess stain. This is when any crackle in the varnish will become apparent.

33 Add a little glitz of Glorious Gold by lightly sliding a popsicle stick loaded with the gold paint along various edges. This should give the effect of paint wearing off and allowing the background gold to show through.

34 When the tray has thoroughly dried, seal it with matte spray sealer.

Victorian Christmas Angels

T his little cherub was inspired by a Christmas card I found in my Great Aunt Pearl's scrapbook. It was postmarked in 1899 and is typical of the art of the Victorian period. I chose to stay with pastel colors for this project, as the Victorian era reminds me of soft, feminine florals and frilly things. These ornaments will add a beautiful Victorian touch to your holiday decor!

Here's a great idea: carry out your Victorian Christmas theme with personalized cards and gift tags. Once you have finished painting your cherub ornament, but before antiquing it, scan it with a color scanner, import it into your favorite design program and make stationery, invitations or super quick ornaments.

Your Victorian Christmas angel theme is limited only by your imagination. Have fun!

MATERIALS

Loew-Cornell Brushes

Series 7300 nos. 4, 6 and 8 shaders

Series 7400 ⅛-inch (3mm) angular shader

Series 7350 no. 2 liner

Series 7000 no. 2 round

Additional Supplies

DecoArt Americana Wood Sealer • DecoArt Americana Faux Glazing Medium • DecoArt Americana Sealer Spray (DAS 13: matte) • DecoArt Perfect Crackle • Tacky Glue • DecoArt Brush 'n Blend Extender • 220-grit sandpaper • graphite paper • tracing paper • Magic Rub® eraser • small scruffy round brush • toothpick • soft lint-free cloth • card stock • tooth-pick • soft lint-free cloth

Surface

Wooden angel ornament from Craine's Cutouts and Crafts

Paint

DecoArt Americana Acrylics, DecoArt Dazzling Metallics (DM)

Base Flesh

Sable Brown

Dark Chocolate

Blue Chiffon

Shading Flesh

Winter Blue

Milk Chocolate

Hi-Lite Flesh

Antique Rose

Wedgewood Blue

Titanium (Snow) White

Antique White

Golden Straw

Jade Green

Light Avocado

Glorious Gold (DM)

Lamp (Ebony) Black

Antique White + Titanium (Snow) White (1:1)

Pattern and Angel Ornament

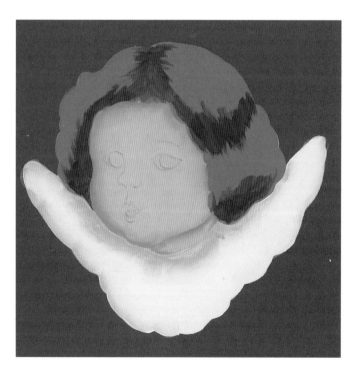

These full-size patterns may be hand-traced or photocopied for personal use only.

1 Lightly sand the wooden ornament to remove any roughness. Apply wood sealer and allow to dry. Using graphite paper and tracing paper, transfer on the outline of the hair and face only. Make registration marks on the pattern and the surface so you can align the pattern again later. Using your no. 6 shader, basecoat the hair with Sable Brown, the face with Base Flesh and the wings with Blue Chiffon. When the hair is dry, stroke in some dark areas using your no. 4 shader and Dark Chocolate, using somewhat of a drybrush effect so you don't have hard lines (see page 11). Stroke in the direction of the hair growth. Using your no. 8 shader, float Shading Flesh around the face and under the jaw. With the same brush, float Winter Blue onto the wings, under the face and hair and on the left edge of the wings.

Angel Ornament, *continued*

2 Using your no. 2 liner and thinned Dark Chocolate, stroke squiggly lines into the hair. Make some lines come down to form light bangs. Follow with another layer of hair, using the Milk Chocolate with the same brush. Reposition the pattern and transfer the rest of the face and the wing feathers. Use your no. 2 round to paint the whites of the eyes with Blue Chiffon; paint the irises using Wedgewood Blue. With the same brush, paint the mouth opening with Dark Chocolate and the lips with Shading Flesh. Use the ⅛-inch (3mm) angular shader to float Winter Blue into the pointed spaces between the feathers. If you so desire, use Brush 'n Blend on your brush to facilitate blending.

Helpful Reminder ~ When using skinny brushes, you need skinny paint! When using liner brushes, you need very thin paint!

3 Add lighter strokes of curled hair using your no. 2 liner with blends of Antique White and Sable Brown. Vary the ratios of these colors to produce random hues. Add the ribbon around the neck, using your no. 2 round and Wedgewood Blue. Follow with a shorter stroke of Winter Blue on top of that, then a stroke or two of Titanium (Snow) White for highlight. Float Shading Flesh onto the upper eyelids using your no. 4 shader. Also float a very narrow float of Shading Flesh around the nose and down to the mouth.

Switch to the no. 2 round. Add tiny lines in Base Flesh for dimples, and add the creases around the nose, upper lip and chin. With the same brush, paint the bottom half of the iris Winter Blue and add the pupil in Lamp (Ebony) Black. Stroke in just a touch of Titanium (Snow) White to suggest teeth (don't try to paint individual teeth). Stroke a thin line of Dark Chocolate over the eye and partially around the bottom lid. Use your Magic Rub® eraser to remove any pattern marks left on the wings. Use the ⅛-inch (3mm) angular shader to highlight the tips of the feathers with Titanium (Snow) White. Float thinned Wedgewood Blue around the neck and under the jaw and hair.

Final Touches

4 Add more strokes of lighter hair strands by adding more Antique White to the Sable Brown and Antique White that you used in step 3 for the hair. Finish the hair by stroking in tiny areas of highlights, with a mix of Antique White and Titanium (Snow) White (1:1).

Use your no. 2 round with thinned Dark Chocolate to stroke in tiny lines to form eyebrows. Use this same loaded brush to paint the very thin crease above the eyelids; also apply very thin eyelashes on the top lid and shorter eyelashes on the bottom.

Still using the same loaded brush, paint two tiny curved lines for nostrils. With the point of the no. 2 round, apply two tiny specks of Titanium (Snow) White as reflected light in the eyes. (Always put the highlights in the same place in each eye. Doing so helps the eyes look like they are fixed in the same direction.)

Use the no. 6 shader to float thinned Base Flesh around the cheeks and just above them. This will make them look chubby.

Add a few strokes of Antique Rose to the lips, followed by tiny strokes of Hi-Lite Flesh for highlighting. Also use Hi-Lite Flesh on the nose, cheeks and chin. (Use very small strokes; don't overdo it!) Reposition the pattern, if needed, and add the stroke flowers (see instructions below). Make a very thin wash of Golden Straw, and apply it all over the hair. This will liven up the hair and give it a bit of luminescence.

Paint the back and edges with two coats of Glorious Gold.

Stroke Flowers

1 Use a no. 6 flat shader double-loaded with Light Avocado and Jade Green to paint pulled leaves (see page 12). Allow to dry.

2 Double load the same brush with Wedgewood Blue and Titanium (Snow) White. With the blue on the outside, make a simple stroke petal by pivoting the chisel edge of the brush on the white and making a tight C-shaped stroke. Turn your work surface, in order to paint the stroke comfortably, as you do each petal. Don't worry about the white center looking messy—it will be fixed. Be sure to paint the background flower first.

3 Paint the other flower, overlapping the first. Then use a very small scruffy round brush to stipple in the center of the flower with Titanium (Snow) White. When that's dry, use a toothpick to dot three dots of Golden Straw onto each flower center.

Crackling

If you plan to make copies of your angel ornament for coordinating items, do so before you crackle the ornament (see ideas for coordinating items below).

Apply DecoArt Perfect Crackle step 1 evenly with a soft brush. Let dry. Apply step 2 the same way, and let dry completely. Small cracks in the finish will appear upon drying.

Let this crackled finish dry for several hours, then antique with a mix of DecoArt Americana Faux Glazing Medium and Glorious Gold (1:1), with a touch of Dark Chocolate added to darken the mixture slightly. The antiquing will emphasize the crackling. Apply with a flat shader and wipe off with a soft lint-free cloth (cotton T-shirt fabric is ideal).

Apply DAS 13:matte spray sealer when antiquing is dry.

Ideas For Coordinating Items

To scan your art, follow the directions for the scanner you are using. If you don't have a scanner, most printing shops have scanning or color printing available for a small price.

After scanning the ornament, I have found it helpful to bump up the saturation by twenty-five percent for printing. When you print, some degree of color is lost, so the increase in saturation will help to compensate for that loss.

Print, then spray the paper with matte spray sealer to seal the color. Allow it to dry before cutting it. Glue it onto the ornament with Tacky Glue.

You can also print the angel onto card stock to make matching holiday cards or gift tags.

Or carry out your theme by painting porcelain ornaments with the colors used on the wooden ornament.

Spray the porcelain ornament with matte spray sealer and let dry. Depending on the surface, you can paint with washes of Winter Blue and Titanium (Snow) White. Trim with Glorious Gold and adorn the ornaments with stroke flowers (see page 134). Apply DecoArt Perfect Crackle and antique as you did for the wooden ornament. You can then hang the ornaments on your tree or wreath with a dainty ribbon.

Be creative and have fun!

QUICK PROJECT 17

New Year's Eve Celebration

Give the party host champagne, wine or sparkling grape juice in this glittering gift box. It's festive and bright, and is sure to make your gift unique. If you are the party host, paint these quick and easy coordinating invitations on blank stationery that you can easily find in your local craft store.

MATERIALS

Loew-Cornell Brushes
Series 7300 no. 4 shader
Series 7051 no. 1 script liner

Additional Supplies
1-inch (25mm) sponge brush
DecoArt Craft Twinkles
DecoArt Americana Spray
  Sealer (DAS 13: matte)
DecoArt Duraclear Varnish
tape
tracing paper
graphite paper

Surface
Papier mâché champagne gift box
Blank white note cards and envelopes from a craft or hobby store

Paint
DecoArt Americana Acrylics, DecoArt Dazzling Metallics (DM), DecoArt Hot Shots (HS)

Glorious Gold (DM)

Venetian Gold (DM)

Bright Green

Lemon Yellow

Electric Pink

Glorious Gold (DM) + Venetian Gold (DM) (1:1)

Thermal Green (HS)

Scorching Yellow (HS)

Sizzling Pink (HS)

Torrid Orange (HS)

Lamp (Ebony) Black

Titanium (Snow) White

Patterns

These full-size patterns may be hand-traced or photocopied for personal use only.

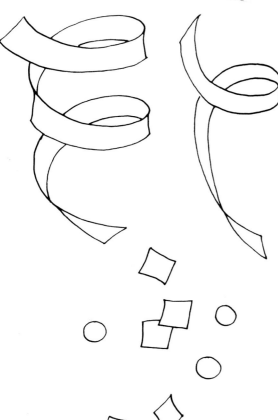

Stripes

1 Basecoat the box with the 1-inch (25mm) sponge brush and two coats of Glorious Gold, allowing it to dry completely between coats and before going on to step 2.

2 Prepare the box by masking with tape that is spaced evenly around the box at an angle (do not stripe the top). The spaces between the strips of tape are the areas that will be painted, creating the stripes.

Burnish (rub) the edges of the tape to prevent bleeding. Apply a thin coat of sealer over the entire area, including the tape. (Applying a coat of sealer over the tape before painting prevents bleeding, and gives you clean edges on the stripes.) Allow to dry before going on to step 3.

3 Mix Glorious Gold with Venetian Gold (1:1), and use your 1-inch (25mm) sponge brush to paint the exposed areas between the tape. Remove the tape when the paint is just about dry.

Streamers and Confetti

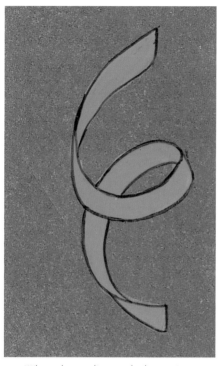

1 Allow the stripes to dry, then use graphite paper and tracing paper to transfer the streamers and confetti pattern onto the box. Leave the lid on and transfer some of the streamers to overlap the lid.

The decorations on the box will be painted randomly, but first all of them need to be undercoated with Titanium (Snow) White using your no. 4 shader.

2 Using the same brush, basecoat the green streamers with Bright Green, the pink ones with Electric Pink and the yellow ones with Lemon Yellow. When dry, paint the green steamers with Thermal Green, the pink with Sizzling Pink and the yellow with Scorching Yellow.

Paint the remaining streamers and confetti with Torrid Orange and Scorching Yellow.

3 When dry, outline each decoration with thinned Lamp (Ebony) Black using the no. 1 script brush. Let dry completely (two hours), then apply varnish. After the varnish dries, apply DecoArt Craft Twinkles.

Invitations

Transfer streamers and confetti randomly around the outside edge of the white card, and the word PARTY to the center. Paint as described above, but eliminate the white undercoat. Outline with Lamp (Ebony) Black.

Do not use varnish on the invitations or envelopes. You may decorate the envelopes with confetti as well, but only on the lower-left corner and the back.

This is another project with which you can be creative, carrying the theme throughout party decorations such as name tags and place cards. See page 135 for more ideas for coordinating items, and instructions for scanning and printing your art. Your creativity is limitless!

Resources

Paints and Mediums
DecoArt, Inc.
Box 327
Stanford, KY 40484
www.decoart.com
(800) 367-3047

Brushes
Loew-Cornell, Inc.
563 Chestnut Ave.
Teaneck, NJ 07666-2491
www.loew-cornell.com
(201) 836-7070
Fax: (201) 836-8110

"The Masters" Brush Cleaner &
Restorer
General Pencil Company
P.O. Box 5311
Redwood City, CA 94063
www.generalpencil.com
(650) 369-4889
Fax: (650) 369-7169

Magic Rub® eraser
Sanford Corporate Headquarters
2711 Washington Blvd.
Bellwood, IL 60104
www.sanford.com
(800) 323-0749

Michaels
8000 Bent Branch Dr.
Irving, TX 75063
www.michaels.com
(800) 642-4235

Liquid Shadow
Kerry Trout
Studio on the Square
59 W. Marion St.
Danville, IN 46122
www.kerrytrout.com

Americana citronella candles
Family Dollar Stores
Executive Offices
P. O. Box 1017
Charlotte, NC 28201-1017
www.familydollar.com
(704) 847-6961

Americana utensil caddy
Country Craft Coop
584 County Road 39
East River Road
Afton, NY 13730
www.countrycraftcoop.com
(607) 639-2834

Autumn Applefest linens & Mother's
Day lace pillows
Jan Brooks Exclusives
33 Russet Rd.
Billerica, MA 01821

Father's Day ("Dad") box
Walnut Hollow® Farm, Inc.
1409 State Road 23
Dodgeville, WI 53533
(800) 950-5101

June Wedding heart porcelain box
J.C.'s Pour 'N More
Joyce Rogers, owner
R.R. 2 Box 227 A
Spearville, KS 67876
(620) 385-2627

New Baby lamp
Linens 'n Things
www.lnt.com
(866) 568-7378

Spring table runner
BagWorks, Inc.
Ft. Worth, TX
www.bagworks.com
(817) 446-8080
(800) 365-7423
Fax: (817) 446-8105
(800) 800-7364

Thanksgiving tray (WD4026)
Stone Bridge Collection
www.4packets.com
(800) 278-8653 (orders only)
(613) 624-5080

Valentine's Day glass candy dish with
lid
Painter's Paradise
Jo C. & Co.
C-10, 950 Ridge Rd.
Claymont, DE 19703
www.paintersparadise.com
(302) 798-3897
Fax: (302) 478-9441

Victorian angel ornaments (bisque)
Bows Plus Bisque
c/o Amy Callihan
24 Augusta Way
N. Chelmsford, MA 01863
www.bowsplusbisque.com
(978) 251-0111

Victorian angel ornaments (wooden)
Craine's Cutouts & Crafts
P. O. Box 306
Haysville, KS 67060
(316) 522-8689

Index

More decorative painting titles from North Light Books!

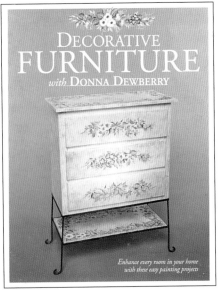

Donna Dewberry shows you how to master her legendary one-stroke technique for painting realistic flowers, fruits and other decorative motifs. Simple step-by-step instructions accompany each project. Guidelines for matching color combinations to existing room schemes enable you to customize every project to fit your décor!

ISBN 1-58180-016-9, paperback, 128 pages, #31662

These books and other fine North Light titles are available from your local art & craft retailer, book store, online supplier or by calling 1-800-448-0915.

With Maureen McNaughton as your coach, you can learn to paint an amazing array of fabulous leaves and flowers with skill and precision. She provides start-to-finish instruction with hundreds of detailed photos. *Beautiful Brushstrokes* is packed with a variety of techniques, from the most basic stroke to more challenging, as well as 5 gorgeous strokework projects.

ISBN 1-58180-381-8, paperback, 128 pages, #32396

Take your decorative painting to an exciting new level of depth and dimension by creating the illusion of reality—one that transforms your work from good to extraordinary! Patti DeRenzo, CDA, shows you how to master the building blocks of realism, value, temperature, intensity and form to render three-dimensional images with height, depth and width.

ISBN 0-89134-995-2, paperback, 128 pages, #31661

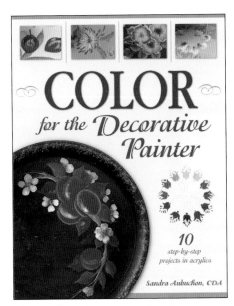

This guide makes using color simple. Best of all, it's as fun as it is instructional, featuring ten step-by-step projects that illustrate color principles in action. As you paint your favorite subjects, you'll learn how to make color work for you. No second-guessing, no regrets-just great-looking paintings and a whole lot of pleasure.

ISBN 1-58180-048-7, paperback, 128 pages, #31796